SQUIRES KITCHEN'S GUIDE TO SUGAR MODELLING

fairytale

Jan Clement-May

FIGURES

First published in March 2016 by
B. Dutton Publishing Limited, The
Grange, Hones Yard, Farnham, Surrey,
GU9 8BB, UK.
Copyright: Jan Clement-May 2016
ISBN-13: 978-1-905113-54-5

Publisher: Beverley Dutton
Group Editor: Jennifer Kelly
Creative Director: Sarah Ryan

Book publishing
Copy Editor: Frankie New
Photography: Alister Thorpe

Magazine publishing
Editor: Jenny Royle
Copy Editor: Adele Duthie
PR and Advertising Manager: Natalie Bull

Printed and bound in China by 1010 Printing Ltd.

Disclaimer

Introduction

Welcome to my third book dedicated to sugar modelling. This time I have given my figures a fantasy theme to build on the skills covered in the previous two books, *Squires Kitchen's Guide to Sugar Animals* and *Squires Kitchen's Guide to Sugar Figures*.

When drawing up the ideas for this book, I let my imagination run wild and tried to put my own twist on some of the world's most-beloved storybook characters. At first glance it may look as though these cake toppers are only for children's cakes, but I hope that these well-known figures will be loved by people of all ages.

From a pretty princess to an ugly ogre, I have included a whole variety of fairytale characters so you can try your hand at modelling both people and animals of all different shapes and sizes. This time all the different pieces you need to assemble each character have been photographed at actual size and numbered to match the step-by-step instructions. These actual-size guides will help you check what you're modelling and give you more confidence as you build each character.

Remember the three Ps when modelling – practice, persistence and lots of patience! It's important to be patient and allow time for the models to dry at certain points so that they don't lose height or shape. Most of all, remember to have fun and use your imagination – I hope you enjoy this book as much as I enjoyed making it!

Jan
x

To my parents, John and Rosina, and my siblings, Julie, Steven, Tracy and Vicky. To my children, Emelia and Christian, along with my very close friends, especially Steph, who have seen a lot of changes in my life recently and have supported and encouraged me unconditionally through the past few years. I thank each and every one of you for being there.

ACKNOWLEDGEMENTS

Thanks to Beverley and Robert Dutton for continuing to believe in my work and for publishing a follow-up to my previous books. A big thank you to the whole publishing team for making the process so smooth and for presenting my work professionally, especially Jenny Kelly, Frankie New and Sarah Ryan, as well as Alister Thorpe for the photography – what a great team!

Contents

Edibles and Equipment

The checklist below is the basic 'toolkit' for the modelling projects throughout this book. Additional items are included at the beginning of each one if anything extra is needed, as are the specific quantities and colours of pastes. Some tools will be used far more than others but all are essential for achieving good-quality results in your edible artwork.

1 Barbecue skewers (wooden)

2 Ball tool

3 Bone tool

4 Cake cards

5 Cranked palette knife

6 Dresden tool

7 Dust food colours (SK)

8 Edible glue (SK)

9 Food colour pens (SK)

10 Non-stick board, small

11 Paintbrushes: nos. 1, 2 and 10

12 Rolling pin, small

13 Scissors

14 Small, sharp knife

15 Spaghetti (raw)

16 Sugar Dough (SK)

17 Sugar Florist Paste/flower paste (SK)

18 White vegetable fat

When making each figure, I find it useful to have a set of digital scales to hand so I can weigh out each piece of paste exactly. I have also included **actual size guides** with every project so you can easily see what size and shape each piece needs to be.

Modelling Basics

Sugar Dough is easy to use and is ideal for modelling animals and figures. These basic hints and tips will ensure you get brilliant results every time!

There are just a few basic shapes in modelling which can then be made into almost anything. From these shapes you can make teardrops, pear shapes, discs or tapered sausages as needed for your sugar models.

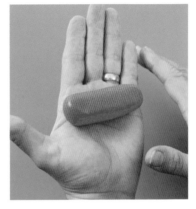

1 **Ball:** roll the paste in the middle of your palms firmly to prevent cracking.

2 **Sausage:** first, roll the paste into a ball then roll back and forth on a work surface to lengthen. Roll just a little to make a short, fat sausage or continue rolling to make a longer, thinner sausage.

3 **Cone:** first, roll the paste into a ball. Place onto a work surface then cup your hands around the ball and turn the paste back and forth. The paste will have a flat base from sitting on the surface and the top should come to a point between your hands.

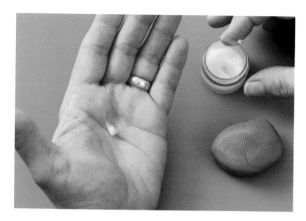

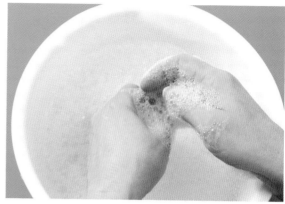

- Rub a little white vegetable fat into your hands before kneading Sugar Dough: this makes it more pliable and less likely to crack, giving a more professional finish to your work. It also prevents the stronger colours from sticking to your hands when working the paste and helps to create an even consistency when adding colour to the paste.

- Wash your hands in warm, soapy water between colour changes and keep your tools clean at all times to prevent small pieces of paste from transferring onto other colours. Make sure that your hands are completely dry before handling the paste otherwise it will become sticky.

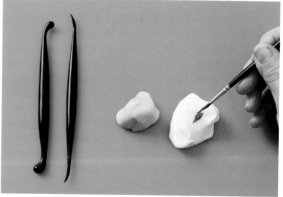

- Use SK Edible Glue to stick pieces together. Using a paintbrush, apply a little glue to the surface of the Sugar Dough before working on the next piece to allow the glue to go tacky. To stick the pieces together, hold them in position for a few moments and support if necessary until they are held together securely.

- If you would like to try working with different flavours, you can use marzipan or Cocoform (modelling chocolate) instead of Sugar Dough. Add paste food colours to create all the colours you need. As both types of paste are very soft, you may not need to use edible glue to stick pieces together.

Marshmallow Rice Cereal

EDIBLES

100g (3½oz) marshmallows

25g (1oz) unsalted butter

75g (2½oz) crisped rice cereal

Makes 200g (7oz)

1 Place the marshmallows and butter in a heavy-based saucepan over a gentle heat. Stir continuously until melted. Leave to cool for a little while.

2 Add the crisped rice cereal to the pan in small amounts, coating the cereal completely with the melted marshmallow mix. Continue until all the crisped rice cereal has been added. Leave to cool before handling.

3 To shape, wrap the amount of marshmallow rice cereal you need in cling film to prevent your hands getting sticky. Shape the mix between your hands, pressing it until it is firm.

4 If you need to insert a skewer into the shape, do so at this stage whilst the mix is still soft enough to push the skewer through.

PROJECTS

DRAGON

EDIBLES

110g (3¾oz) marshmallow
rice cereal mix (see recipe on
page 10)

SK Sugar Dough:

   175g (6oz) Red

   60g (2oz) Yellow

   25g (just over ¾oz) Orange

   1g (small pinch) White

   1g (small pinch) Black

EQUIPMENT

Basic equipment (see pages
6 to 7)

1 x 18cm and 2 x 5.5cm
(2¼" and 7") long wooden
barbecue skewers

Tweezers (for sugarcraft use
only) (optional)

1 Model the marshmallow rice cereal mix into the shape of
the dragon's body following the size guide and leave to
cool completely (see page 10). Push the 18cm (7") barbecue
skewer down through the top of the body, leaving 4cm (1½")
protruding from the base.

2 Roll out 6g (just under ¼oz) of Orange Sugar Dough for
each wing, leaving one side thick enough for a skewer.
Brush the shorter skewers with a little edible glue and gently
insert them partway into the side of the wings. Cut the wings

Important note: Remember to remove the
barbecue skewers before the model is eaten.

to shape with a small knife following the size guide and vein with a Dresden tool. Bring the top of each wing to a point, bend gently and leave to dry.

3 Roll out 50g (1¾oz) of Yellow Sugar Dough into a long triangle, following the size guide. Attach to the front of the body and smooth over the surface with your fingers. Draw lines across the paste with a Dresden tool then add a few creases on either side. Roll out 120g (4¼oz) of Red Sugar Dough and cover the rest of the body, butting the red paste up against the yellow.

4 Roll 25g (just over ¾oz) of Red Sugar Dough into a cone for the tail, push your thumb into the wider end and pinch the paste between your finger and thumb to hollow it out. Attach to the back of the dragon with edible glue and smooth over the join with a Dresden tool.

5 Pinch out tiny balls from 5g (just under ¼oz) of Yellow Sugar Dough and stick them over the dragon's back. Use 3g (⅛oz) of Orange Sugar Dough to make small triangular spines in varying sizes and attach them in a row down the dragon's back and tail with edible glue.

6 Shape 1g (small pinch) of Orange Sugar Dough into a triangle with pointed corners, then push a paintbrush handle into the base to help attach it to the tail. Secure it to the end of the tail with edible glue and bend the tip over a little.

7 Roll a 25g (just over ¾oz) sausage of Red Sugar Dough for each back leg, following the size guide. Bend the legs and mark three claw holes in the end of each foot with a paintbrush handle. Attach the back legs to either side of the body with edible glue and smooth over the joins with a Dresden tool.

8 Roll a 10g (¼oz) sausage of Red Sugar Dough for each arm, following the size guide. Bend slightly, mark on creases with a Dresden tool and make holes in the same way as for the back feet. Secure in position with edible glue, so one hand rests on top of the other. Use a Dresden tool to smooth the paste from the arms onto the body.

9 For the claws, pinch out 12 tiny balls from 1g (small pinch) of Orange Sugar Dough, roll each ball into a point and secure inside the holes in the back feet and hands with edible glue.

10 Make two equal balls from 1g (small pinch) of Orange Sugar Dough. Push a spare wooden skewer into the dragon's back at the points where you will attach the wings, then remove. Attach the balls over the holes and make a hole in each ball with a skewer. Push the skewered wings into the holes and secure with edible glue, using a pair of tweezers to help position them.

11 Roll 8g (¼oz) of Red Sugar Dough into a ball for the neck, gently squeeze it between your finger and

thumb then push a spare skewer through the centre to make a ring. Mark two lines around the ring with a Dresden tool, then secure over the skewer at the top of the body using edible glue.

12 For the head, shape 45g (1½oz) of Red Sugar Dough into a thick sausage following the size guide. Gently pull the paste down a little at the front end to form the top lip. Mark the mouth with the blunt edge of a small knife then add dimples with the end of a paintbrush. Push a Dresden tool into either side of the mouth where the teeth will be attached.

13 Gently squeeze the middle of the head to make a small indent and give it shape. Push a paintbrush handle into the nose to make two nostrils, then mark around them with a Dresden tool. Push a spare skewer into the base of the head at an angle, remove and attach to the skewered neck with edible glue. Push the end of a paintbrush into either side of the head where the yellow spikes will be attached.

14 Pinch out two small balls of White Sugar Dough for the teeth and shape into pointed sausages. Secure inside the holes in the mouth with edible glue, bending them slightly.

15 Roll a 3g (⅛oz) ball of Red Sugar Dough for each eye and attach to the top of the head. Attach two small discs of White Sugar Dough to the front of each eye, then secure two smaller discs of Yellow Sugar Dough on top. Roll two tiny sausages of Black Sugar Dough and attach to the yellow discs.

16 Cut out two thin eyelashes from the remaining Black Sugar Dough and carefully attach to the top of each eye with edible glue. Make a slight dent in each eye with a Dresden tool, brush with a little edible glue and attach two tiny white highlights.

17 Make four equal pieces from 1g (small pinch) of Yellow Sugar Dough for the yellow spikes. Roll each piece into a tapered sausage and secure in the holes behind the mouth with edible glue.

18 Shape 1g (small pinch) of Red Sugar Dough into a cone for each ear, flatten slightly then wrap around a paintbrush handle to shape. Pinch the paste at the tip, trim if necessary and attach to either side of the head with edible glue. Make several small spines from 3g (⅛oz) of Orange Sugar Dough and attach them down the back of the dragon's head and neck to finish.

DRAGON
SIZE GUIDE

1

3

2

10

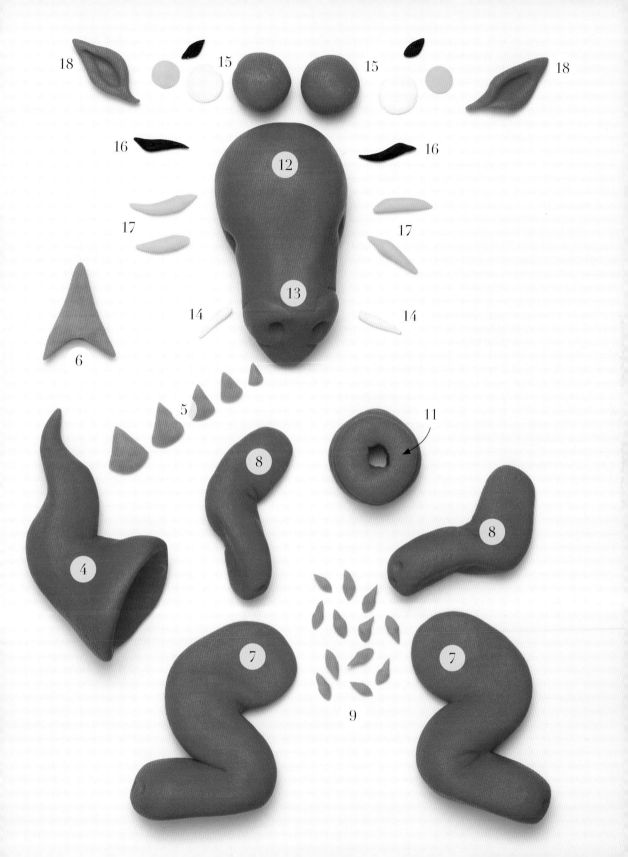

PRINCESS AND FROG

EDIBLES

130g (4½oz) marshmallow rice cereal mix (see recipe on page 10)

SK Sugar Dough:

175g (6oz) pale blue (White + pinch of Blue)

30g (1oz) Soft Beige

30g (1oz) Yellow

12g (½oz) pink (White + pinch of Red)

8g (¼oz) Black

6g (just under ¼oz) light green (5g (just under ¼oz) White + 1g (small pinch) Green)

5g (just under ¼oz) White

3g (⅛oz) Green

1g (small pinch) Brown

1g (small pinch) lime green (Yellow + Green)

SK Ice White Designer Fairy Sparkles Dust Food Colour

SK Professional Food Colour Pens: Black and Red

EQUIPMENT

Basic equipment (see pages 6 to 7)

15cm (6") long wooden barbecue skewer

Important note: Remember to remove the barbecue skewer before the model is eaten.

PRINCESS

1 Following the size guide, model the marshmallow rice cereal mix into the shape of the princess' skirt with two indents at the front for the legs (see page 10). Leave to cool completely.

2 Roll out 8g (¼oz) of Black Sugar Dough and cut out two rounded triangles of different sizes, following the size guide. Attach over the indents in the front of the marshmallow rice cereal skirt with a little edible glue.

3 For the shoes, divide 1g (small pinch) of White Sugar Dough in half and shape each piece into an oval. Push the end of a bone tool into the top of each one and set aside.

4 Roll a 2g (pinch) sausage of Soft Beige Sugar Dough for each leg, shaping one end to fit inside the shoes. Secure the legs to the shoes with edible glue then gently narrow the ankles on both legs. Attach the top of the legs to the black paste with the shoes resting at a slight angle, as if on heels.

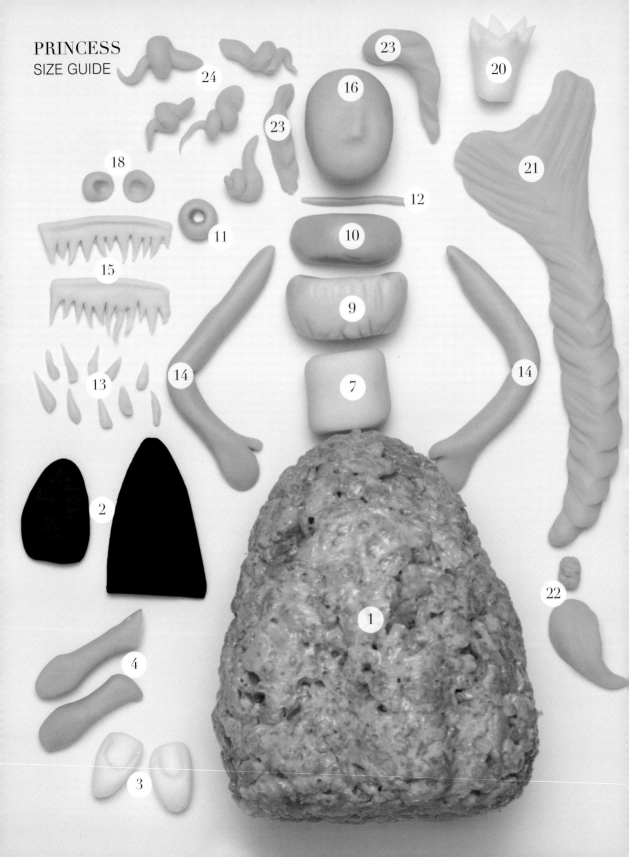

PRINCESS
SIZE GUIDE

5 Push the barbecue skewer down through the centre of the marshmallow rice cereal skirt: you can hold onto this whilst securing sections of paste to the skirt. Roll out 160g (5½oz) of pale blue Sugar Dough, cut out triangular sections in manageable sizes and attach them to the sides of the marshmallow rice cereal skirt. Start on one side of the black triangles and work all the way around the skirt until you reach the other side. Run a Dresden tool randomly up and down the sections to mark on folds. Cut another section to fit between the black triangles and texture the paste so it looks gathered in the middle.

6 Knead together the pale blue Sugar Dough trimmings and divide in half. Roll one section into a sausage, flatten it into a strip and cut a straight edge along one side. Concertina the paste to form the ruffled fabric over one of the legs. Cut to size and attach to the skirt with edible glue, smoothing the paste onto the skirt with a Dresden tool. Make another fabric section in the same way to fit over the other leg.

7 Reserve a small pinch from 10g (¼oz) of pink Sugar Dough and roll the remaining paste into a ball. Flatten the top and bottom and squeeze the paste a little in the middle to make the corset. Mark the front opening with the blunt edge of a knife and mark eyelets down either side with the end of a Dresden tool. Make a hole down the middle of the corset with a spare skewer then secure the corset over the skewered skirt.

8 Roll the reserved pinch of pink Sugar Dough into a very thin sausage, then brush a little edible glue in each of the holes on the corset. Cut small sections off the length of

paste and secure them between the holes, starting at the top and working down. Cut the remaining paste in half, form each piece into a loop and secure to the bottom of the corset with edible glue.

9 Shape 10g (¼oz) of pale blue Sugar Dough into an oval for the bust then pinch up the paste a little across the top and add creases with a Dresden tool. Make a hole through the centre with a spare skewer and attach over the skewered corset with edible glue.

10 Shape 4g (just under ¼oz) of Soft Beige Sugar Dough into a slight dome and gently squeeze across the top to make the shoulders. Make a hole through the middle of the paste with a spare skewer then secure over the skewered dress: the shoulders should fit inside the top of the dress.

11 Roll a small ball of Soft Beige Sugar Dough for the neck, make a hole through the centre with a spare skewer and attach over the skewered shoulders.

12 Roll a small amount of pink Sugar Dough into a very thin sausage for the choker, brush a little edible glue around the base of the neck and attach the sausage around it. Cut to size and stick the ends down.

13 Pinch out 10 very small pieces of pale blue Sugar Dough and shape them into points. Attach them across the top of the dress with edible glue and secure in place with a Dresden tool.

14 For the arms, roll 10g (¼oz) of Soft Beige Sugar Dough into a long sausage and pinch the ends between your finger and thumb to flatten the hands. Twist the paste just above the hands to make the wrists and keep the arms smooth. Make a small cut on the inside of each hand, ease out the thumbs and smooth over any cut edges. Cut the top of the arms at an angle to fit against the shoulders and cut to size if necessary, following the size guide. Mark the elbows with a Dresden tool and bend slightly. Secure the arms to the shoulders and position the hands over the ruffled sections of the dress with edible glue.

15 Roll out 2g (pinch) of pale blue Sugar Dough, cut out two zigzag-shaped sleeves following the size guide then run the blunt edge of the knife just under the straight edge. Secure the sleeves around each arm with edible glue and cut to size if necessary.

16 Reserve two small pieces from 12g (just under ½oz) of Soft Beige Sugar Dough and roll the remaining paste into an oval for the head. Push the end of a spare skewer into the base and rest it in the palm of your hand while you add the facial features. Use a bone tool to lift up the paste in the centre of the face to make the nose. Push in either side just above the nose to form the bridge and continue until a small nose has formed. Push the end of a Dresden tool into the base of the nose to make two nostrils.

17 Mark the mouth opening with a Dresden tool then run a bone tool underneath it to form a bottom lip. Run your finger over any grooves in the paste then push a bone tool into the corners of the mouth to add dimples. Use a bone tool to make small indents for the eyes. Remove the skewer then attach the head over the skewered neck with edible glue.

18 Roll the reserved paste into two balls for the ears, then brush a little edible glue on either side of the head level with the nose. Push the end of a bone tool into the balls and attach to either side of the head, smoothing over the paste at the front with a bone tool.

19 Draw inside the eye sockets with a black food colour pen, add a couple of eyelashes at the sides and draw on the eyebrows. Secure a disc of White Sugar Dough inside each eye socket with edible glue. Attach very small discs of Brown Sugar Dough on top, then add two smaller black discs for the pupils. Make a small dent in each eye with a Dresden tool, brush with a little edible glue and add tiny white highlights. Draw over the lips using a red food colour pen then soften the colour with a damp paintbrush.

20 Roll 3g (⅛oz) of White Sugar Dough into a cone for the crown then push a paintbrush into the wider end to make an opening in the top. Cut V-shapes out of the top edge with a sharp knife, smooth over the cut edges and trim the base. Set aside.

21 Roll 15g (½oz) of Yellow Sugar Dough into a long cone for the plait and flatten the paste at the top end following the size guide. Working down from the top of the plait, mark gentle indents on either side of the paste at equal points. Attach the plait to the back of the head and down the back of the dress so it curls a little at the base.

22 Shape 2g (pinch) of Yellow Sugar Dough into a cone, mark lines down it with a Dresden tool then bring the end to a point. Attach it to the dress at the bottom of the plait with edible glue. Attach a small ball of pink Sugar Dough between the main plait and the end of the plait then add creases with a Dresden tool.

23 Divide 5g (just under ¼oz) of Yellow Sugar Dough into two unequal pieces, shape them into cones and slightly flatten each piece. Add hair lines with a Dresden tool and attach to the sides of the head with edible glue. Attach the crown to the head with edible glue. Divide 5g (just under ¼oz) of Yellow Sugar Dough into two parts and shape them into cones. Add hair lines with a Dresden tool and attach around the side of the head.

24 Make several thin, long cone shapes from 10g (¼oz) of Yellow Sugar Dough and curl them around on themselves to make locks of hair. Use edible glue to attach a few around the base of the fringe, behind the ears, around the crown and over the back of the hair. Secure each piece to the head with edible glue.

25 Brush Ice White dust food colour over the dress details and the crown to add a magical sparkle to the princess.

FROG

26 Roll out the light green Sugar Dough and cut out the lily pad following the size guide below. Use a Dresden tool to mark lines outwards from the indent in the lily pad and set aside.

27 Divide 1g (small pinch) of Green Sugar Dough into four equal parts, roll each piece into a ball then flatten them between your finger and thumb. Attach two discs of paste to the top of the lily pad with edible glue and set the other two aside.

28 Shape 3g (⅛oz) of Green Sugar Dough into a pear shape for the frog's body. Pinch out two small pieces of lime green Sugar Dough for the eyes and set aside. Shape the remaining lime green Sugar Dough into a slightly smaller pear shape to stick over the front of the body and secure in place with edible glue. Attach the body over the feet on the lily pad and attach the two reserved green discs to either side of the body with edible glue.

29 Attach the eyes to the top of the body and add the pupils with the tip of a black food colour pen.

FROG
SIZE GUIDE

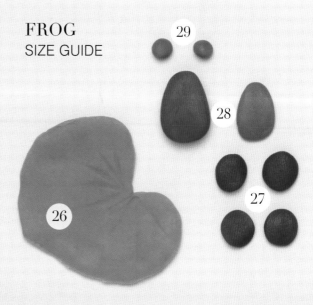

KNIGHT

EDIBLES

SK Sugar Dough:

  130g (4½oz) grey (White
  and pinch of Black)

  20g (¾oz) Brown

  16g (½oz) Soft Beige

  15g (½oz) Black

  5g (just under ¼oz) Red

  1g (small pinch) Green

  1g (small pinch) White

SK Black Professional Food
Colour Pen

SK Black Quality Food Colour
(QFC) Paste

EQUIPMENT

Basic equipment (see
pages 6 to 7)

18cm and 21.5cm (7" and
8½") long wooden barbecue
skewers

1 For the spearhead, shape 4g (just under ¼oz) of grey
Sugar Dough into a cone and flatten it slightly. Dip the
18cm (7") skewer into edible glue then push it into the end
of the cone. Mark both sides of the spearhead with the blunt
edge of a knife.

2 Make the band at the base of the spearhead from 1g
(small pinch) of Brown Sugar Dough, then feed it up the
skewer and secure under the spearhead. Mark across the
paste with a Dresden tool. Mix some black paste food colour
with a little cooled, boiled water and paint the skewer black.
Set aside to dry.

3 Using 10g (¼oz) of grey Sugar Dough for each shoe,
shape each piece into a cone and mark a line down the
centre of the shoes with the blunt edge of a knife. Use a spare
skewer to make a hole towards the back of one of the shoes.

4 Roll 40g (1½oz) of grey Sugar Dough into a sausage
for the legs. Roll the paste either side of the middle
to lengthen and narrow the legs a little whilst keeping the
thickness of the hips in the centre, then bend the sausage in
half. Dip the end of the 21.5cm (8½") skewer into edible glue
and gently insert it through the hips and down one leg using a
twisting motion. Insert the skewer protruding from the leg into

Important note: Remember to remove the barbecue
skewers before the model is eaten.

KNIGHT
SIZE GUIDE

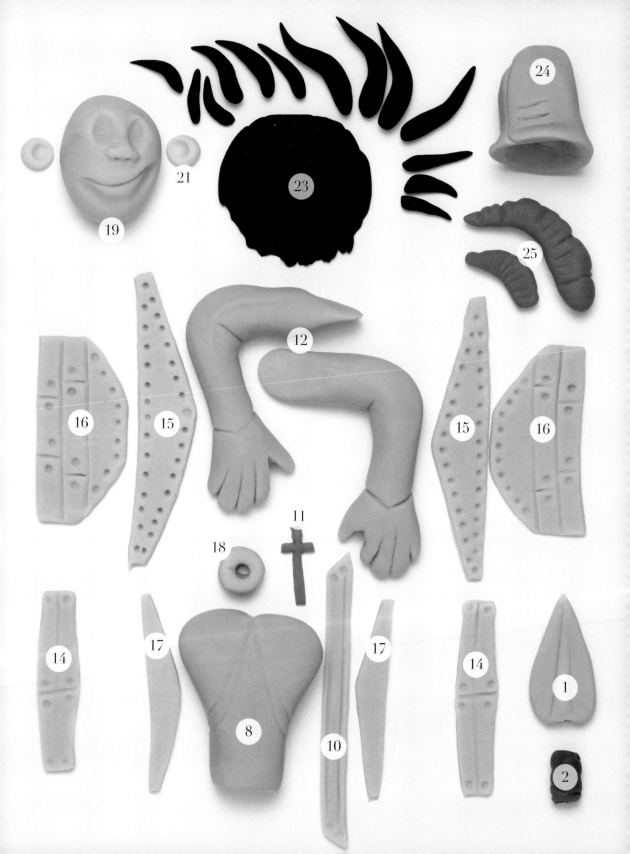

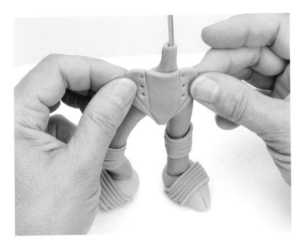

the top of the shoe and secure with edible glue. Pinch up the paste from the hips around the skewer to secure it in place. Add lines across the top of the legs with the blunt edge of a knife. Secure the second shoe to the other leg with edible glue, then bend the leg slightly. Leave to dry.

5 Roll out 2g (pinch) of grey Sugar Dough and cut out two rectangles to fit over the shoes following the size guide. Cut the sides at an angle and mark lines over the top with the blunt edge of a knife. Secure to the shoes and push the end of a paintbrush into the corners.

6 For the armour over the knees, roll out 4g (just under ¼oz) of grey Sugar Dough and cut out four strips following the size guide. Indent the outline of the two angled pieces with the blunt edge of a knife and mark rivets in the ends with a paintbrush handle. Secure around the knees with edible glue. Mark a central line across the remaining two pieces then add rivets as before. Secure to the knees just below the first pieces with edible glue.

7 Roll out 6g (just under ¼oz) of grey Sugar Dough and cut out two pieces of armour to cover the hips. Mark lines over them with the blunt edge of a knife and add rivets with a paintbrush handle. Attach to the front and back of the hips with edible glue.

8 Roll 12g (just under ½oz) of grey Sugar Dough into a thick sausage and flatten the top to make the torso, following the size guide. Mark lines from the top to the sides of the torso with the blunt edge of a knife. Make a hole down

through the torso with a spare skewer and secure over the hips with edible glue.

9 For the cape, roll out 20g (¾oz) of Brown Sugar Dough into a rectangle, add creases with a Dresden tool and gather the paste a little at the top. Make a few cuts across the base of the cape to make the edges look ragged then attach around the back of the waist. Lift one side slightly, support the paste with kitchen paper and leave to dry.

10 Roll 2g (small pinch) of grey Sugar Dough into a sausage, flatten it down and cut a strip to fit around the waist. Cut the ends at an angle so they fit neatly together. Make indents along the sides with the blunt edge of a knife and secure around the waist with edible glue. Push a paintbrush handle into the joins to create rivets.

11 Roll out 1g (small pinch) of Red Sugar Dough and cut out a cross using a small, sharp knife. Attach to the front of the body with edible glue.

12 For each arm, roll a sausage from 9g (¼oz) of grey Sugar Dough that is slightly larger at one end. Pinch the larger end to flatten it slightly for the hand then make a cut in one side with a small knife to bring out the thumb. Smooth over the cut edge and use a knife to mark out the rest of the fingers. Mark lines across the wrists with the blunt edge of a knife. Mark the elbows with a Dresden tool, bend the arms slightly and pinch the shoulders between your finger and thumb to fit them to the body.

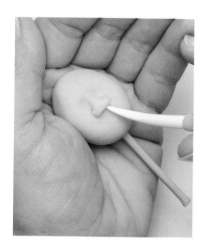

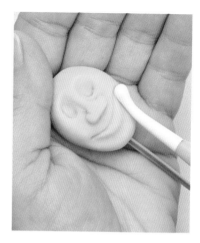

13 Secure one arm to the body with edible glue and rest the hand in front of the hips. Attach the second arm and secure the spear inside the hand with edible glue. Secure the base of the spear to the side of the foot with a small amount of grey Sugar Dough to prevent it moving around and damaging the arm. Support the arm with rolled kitchen paper until completely dry.

14 Roll out 2g (pinch) of grey Sugar Dough and cut out two rectangles following the size guide. Mark vertical and horizontal lines across each piece of paste then use a paintbrush handle to add the rivets. Secure around the elbows with edible glue.

15 Roll out 3g (just under ¼oz) of grey Sugar Dough and cut out two long, triangular pieces following the size guide. Use the end of a paintbrush to mark rivets around the edge of each piece, then attach them over the top of the shoulders.

16 Roll out another 3g (just under ¼oz) of grey Sugar Dough and cut out two pieces of armour to cover the upper arms, following the size guide. Mark horizontal and vertical lines across each piece with the blunt edge of a knife and use the end of a paintbrush to add rivets. Use edible glue to attach them around the upper arms so they are touching the shoulder pieces.

17 Roll out 2g (pinch) of grey Sugar Dough and cut out two long, thin triangular pieces following the size

guide. Attach them around the wrists with edible glue so the angled side points down towards the hands then add rivets at the join.

18 For the neck, shape 1g (small pinch) of grey Sugar Dough into a disc and make a hole through the centre with a spare skewer. Secure to the top of the skewered torso with edible glue.

19 Roll 15g (½oz) of Soft Beige Sugar Dough into an oval for the head, push a spare skewer into the base and rest it in the palm of your hand while you create the facial features. Use a bone tool to lift up the paste in the centre of the face to make the nose and smooth over any grooves with your finger. Shape the nose with a Dresden tool and push the tip into the end of the nose to make the nostrils. Indent the eye sockets with a bone tool and shape with a Dresden tool.

20 Use the Dresden tool to mark the mouth opening so it is slightly raised on one side. Run the bone tool underneath the opening to form a bottom lip and smooth over any grooves with your finger. Push the bone tool into the corners of the mouth to add dimples and mark lines on either side of the nose with the Dresden tool. Remove the skewer and secure the head over the skewered neck with edible glue.

21 Divide 1g (small pinch) of Soft Beige Sugar Dough into two equal balls for the ears, then brush a little edible glue on either side of the head level with the nose.

Push a bone tool into each ear and attach to either side of the head. Smooth over the Sugar Dough at the front of each ear to blend it into the head.

22 Run a black food colour pen around the edge of each eye socket to define the eyes. Secure a small ball of White Sugar Dough into each socket, attach a small disc of Green Sugar Dough on top and a smaller black disc for the pupil. Make a small dent in each eye with a Dresden tool, brush with a little edible glue and add a tiny piece of white paste for the highlight. Use a black food colour pen to draw on the raised eyebrows.

23 Shape 6g (just under ¼oz) of Black Sugar Dough into a disc that fits over the back of the head, add hair lines with a Dresden tool and secure in place with edible glue. Shape two small triangles for the sideburns, add texture and secure in front of each ear. Use a Dresden tool to smooth the sideburns into the rest of the hair. Shape the remaining Black Sugar Dough into different-sized cones, add texture with a Dresden tool and attach to the top of the head to make a sweeping fringe.

24 Shape 10g (¼oz) of grey Sugar Dough into a rounded cone for the helmet, push your thumb into the underside and pinch the paste out a little at the base. Mark lines over the front of the helmet with the blunt edge of a small knife.

25 Roll 1g (small pinch) of Red Sugar Dough into a sausage that tapers towards one end. Mark lines over both sides with a Dresden tool and attach to the top of the helmet with edible glue. Make a larger piece in the same way from 3g (⅛oz) of Red Sugar Dough and secure over the first section so it overhangs slightly at the front.

WIZARD

WIZARD
SIZE GUIDE

EDIBLES

SK Sugar Dough:

130g (just over 4½oz) Brown

25g (just over ¾oz) Soft Beige

20g (¾oz) Black

15g (½oz) grey (White + pinch of Black)

10g (¼oz) Golden Bear Brown

1g (small pinch) White

SK Black Professional Food Colour Pen

SK Pastel Pink Designer Pastel Dust Food Colour

Important note: Remember to remove the inedible supports before the model is eaten.

EQUIPMENT

Basic equipment (see pages 6 to 7)

9cm and 20cm (3½" and 8") long wooden barbecue skewers

5cm (2") length of raw, dried spaghetti

4.5cm (1¾") round cutter

1 For the glasses, roll a small pinch of Black Sugar Dough into a thin, 5cm (2") long sausage. Bend the ends round to make two circles, following the size guide, and secure with edible glue. Set aside to dry.

2 Roll a sausage from 5g (just under ¼oz) of Golden Bear Brown Sugar Dough for the wizard's staff. Dip the end of the 9cm (3½") skewer into edible glue then push it down into the paste very roughly. Twist the paste at the top a little and make the staff narrower at the base. Set aside to dry.

3 For the wand, colour the spaghetti strand with a black food colour pen and set aside.

4 Shape a cone from 6g (just under ¼oz) of Brown Sugar Dough for each shoe, mark creases on the sides with a Dresden tool and turn the points upward a little. Set aside.

5 Roll 60g (2oz) of Brown Sugar Dough into a sausage then push your thumb into the end of the paste and pinch out the edges to create a hollow. Push the 20cm (8") skewer down through the top of the brown robe, leaving 5cm (2") protruding from the base, then pinch the paste around the skewer at the top. Place the robe over the shoes so they are positioned apart, then secure the shoes to the base of the robe with edible glue. Mark rough creases over the robe with a Dresden tool and leave to dry.

6 Shape 30g (1oz) of Brown Sugar Dough into a rounded cone for the body following the size guide. Push a spare

skewer down the centre of the paste from the top to make a hole, then push a paintbrush handle into the thicker end to widen it so that it fits over the robe. Secure in place with edible glue, mark on creases and open up the neck area a little with a Dresden tool.

7 Roll out 4g (just under ¼oz) of Golden Bear Brown Sugar Dough into a long sausage for the belt. Brush edible glue around the waist, attach the belt and cut to size. Cut a small piece off the end of the leftover paste and set aside. Roll the cut end of the leftover paste to a point, bend in half and attach to the end of the belt so it hangs down the body. Secure the small section over the join to make the knot.

8 For the key and chain, pinch out two small balls from 2g (pinch) of grey Sugar Dough. Roll each ball into small lengths for the chain loops and set aside. Shape the remaining paste into a small, thick sausage and flatten slightly to make the key. Make a hole in the top of the key with the end of a paintbrush. Flatten the sides of the key shank then trim to size, leaving a small section at the end. Add detail to the key with a Dresden tool. Thread one loop through the hole in the key and stick the ends together, then secure the second loop through the first and attach to the belt with edible glue.

9 Roll 1g (small pinch) of Soft Beige Sugar Dough into a small cone for the neck then push a spare skewer through the centre to make a hole. Secure the neck over the skewered body with edible glue and ease the paste into the opening.

10 Roll out 3g (⅛oz) of Brown Sugar Dough, cut out the collar following the size guide and secure in place with edible glue.

11 Roll 12g (just under ½oz) of Brown Sugar Dough into a cone for each arm. Push your thumb into the wider end and gently pinch out the paste to create long sleeves. Flatten each arm slightly, mark on the elbows and add creases with a Dresden tool. Secure to either side of the body with edible glue, bringing the arms to the front. Press the top of the sleeves with a Dresden tool to secure in place. Secure the walking stick between the sleeves with edible glue.

12 Shape 2g (pinch) of Soft Beige Sugar Dough into a cone for each hand and flatten slightly. Make a

cut in one side of the hand and ease out the thumb. Make three indents with a sharp knife to create the fingers. Secure the end of the coloured spaghetti inside the first hand, wrap the fingers around it a little and set aside. Make the second hand in the same way but ease out a little finger as well as a thumb. Use edible glue to secure the second hand inside a sleeve and over the top of the walking stick. Secure the hand holding the wand into the other sleeve, resting it on top of the first hand.

13 Shape 15g (½oz) of Soft Beige Sugar Dough into an oval, push a spare skewer into the base and rest the head in the palm of your hand while you work on it. Mark the mouth opening with a Dresden tool, then turn the tool upwards and lift the paste along the opening to form the top lip. Turn the tool downwards and bring out a bottom lip in the same way. Push a bone tool inside the mouth to open it up a little more and smooth over it carefully. Run a bone tool under the bottom lip and smooth over any grooves with your finger. Push a bone tool into either side of the mouth to form dimples then gently squeeze the sides of the head to make small cheeks. Attach a small pinch of Black Sugar Dough inside the mouth and smooth over with a Dresden tool.

14 Roll 1g (small pinch) of Soft Beige Sugar Dough into a ball for the nose and secure above the mouth with edible glue, merging the paste onto the head with a Dresden tool. Push the end of a paintbrush into the nose to make nostrils then define the sides of the nose with a Dresden tool. Run the Dresden tool from the nose to the cheeks to create smile lines.

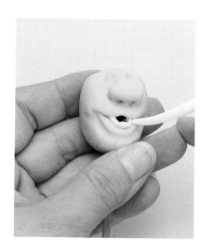
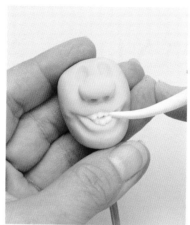
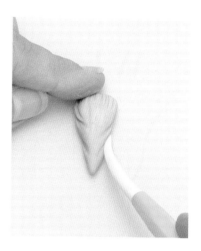

15 To make the teeth, roll out a small amount of White Sugar Dough, cut it in half horizontally and divide into sections with a knife. Push a Dresden tool into the paste a little to define each tooth. Brush edible glue inside the bottom lip and attach a row of teeth, cutting to size if necessary. Tuck the ends to the back of the mouth with a Dresden tool. Attach the top teeth in the same way, making sure the two front teeth are central.

16 Make two indents for the eyes with a bone tool then outline the sockets with a black food colour pen. Secure a small disc of White Sugar Dough inside each eye socket with edible glue. Attach two very small discs of Golden Bear Brown Sugar Dough on top, then add two smaller Black discs for the pupils. Make a small dent in each eye with a Dresden tool, brush with a little edible glue and add tiny white highlights. Remove the skewer and attach the head over the neck with edible glue.

17 For the ears, brush edible glue on either side of the head and roll two small balls of Soft Beige Sugar Dough. Indent each ball with the end of a bone tool and secure to the sides of the head, smoothing over the paste at the front.

18 Roll two small sausages of grey Sugar Dough for the eyebrows and secure in place, texturing the paste with the end of a Dresden tool.

19 Shape 2g (pinch) of grey Sugar Dough into a cone for the beard, flatten it down and add texture with a Dresden tool. Cut a straight edge at the thicker end and secure to the chin with edible glue. Push the paste onto the head with a Dresden tool.

20 Take 8g (¼oz) of grey Sugar Dough and pinch out four small balls for the hair around the ears and a slightly bigger ball for the fringe. Roll the remaining paste into a sausage, flatten it slightly and texture it with a Dresden tool. Attach around the back of the head with edible glue, smoothing the top of the hair onto the head with a Dresden tool. Shape two small balls into triangles, add texture and secure in front of each ear. Shape the other two balls so they fit just below the ears, secure and texture as before. Add the final piece of paste at the front of the head to make the fringe and texture as before.

21 Roll out 5g (just under ¼oz) of Black Sugar Dough and cut out a circle with the round cutter. Smooth over the edges and attach to the top of the head, covering any Soft Beige Sugar Dough still showing. Shape 12g (just under ½oz) of Black Sugar Dough into a long cone, flatten the wider end on the work surface and attach to the top of the disc with edible glue. Bend the tip of the hat back on itself a little.

22 Brush a little Pastel Pink dust food colour over the top of the nose and cheeks and attach the glasses with edible glue.

WITCH AND BLACK CAT

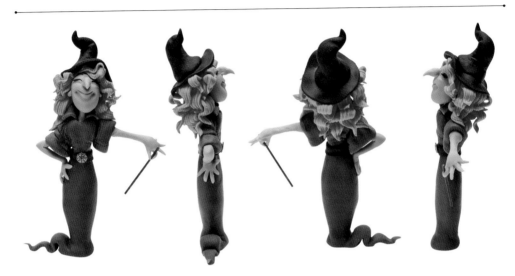

EDIBLES

SK Sugar Dough:

85g (2¾oz) purple (White + SK Professional Violet Dust Food Colour)

65g (2¼oz) Black

30g (1oz) Red

20g (¾oz) (12g Green + 8g White)

1g (small pinch) White

SK Black Professional Food Colour Pen

Important note: Please remember to remove the inedible supports before the models are eaten.

EQUIPMENT

Basic equipment (see pages 6 to 7)

6.5cm, 10.5cm and 20cm (2½", 4¼" and 8") long wooden barbecue skewers

2.5cm and 5cm (1" and 2") long strands of dried, raw spaghetti

5cm (2") round cutter

Drinking straw

WITCH

1 To make the witch's wand, colour the 5cm (2") long piece of dried spaghetti with a black food colour pen and set aside.

2 Shape 55g (2oz) of purple Sugar Dough into a long sausage for the skirt. Squeeze the waist a little at the top and shape the other end into a long point. Bend 7.5cm (3") from the pointed end, flatten the base on a work surface and squeeze the paste just above the bottom of the skirt. Concertina the pointed end a little then push the 20cm (8") long skewer down the centre of the skirt, leaving 5cm (2") protruding from the base. Squeeze the paste around the skewer a little to secure it in place.

3 Shape 12g (just under ½oz) of purple Sugar Dough into a pear shape for the bodice, then push your thumb into the smaller end and pinch out the paste a little to form a hollow. Push a bone tool into the opposite end to make an indent for the neck. Push a spare skewer through the centre of the bodice to make a hole and attach it to the top of the skirt with edible glue. Smooth over the paste at the join with a Dresden tool.

WITCH
SIZE GUIDE

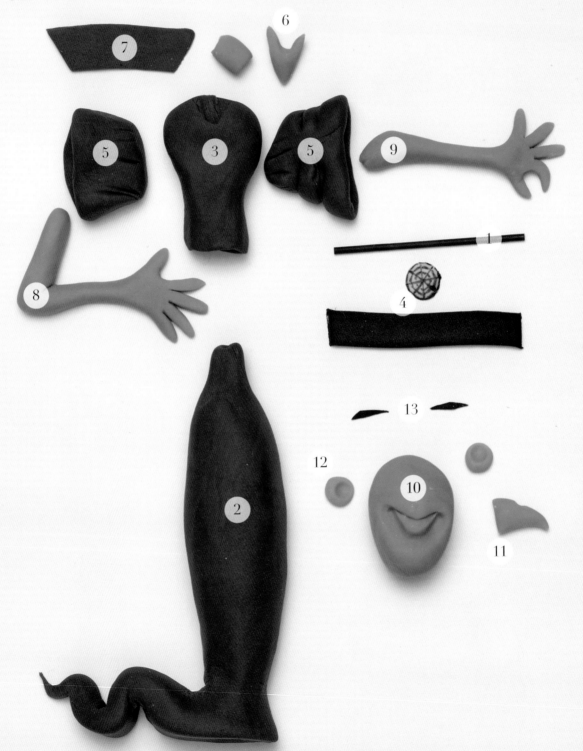

4 Roll 2g (pinch) of Black Sugar Dough into a sausage for the belt, flatten it down and cut a 1cm (³/₈") wide strip following the size guide. Attach it around the waist with edible glue. Flatten down the pinch of White Sugar Dough then draw a spider's web on the surface with a black food colour pen. Attach to the front of the belt with edible glue.

5 Shape 6g (just under ¼oz) of purple Sugar Dough into a cone for one of the sleeves, push your thumb into the wider end and pinch the paste between your finger and thumb to open up the end. Mark creases over the sleeve with a Dresden tool, secure to the side of the body with edible glue and merge the paste with a Dresden tool. Make the second sleeve in the same way, secure to the body and make a hole in the end with a spare skewer.

6 Divide 1g (small pinch) of Green Sugar Dough in half, shape one piece into a V-shape for the witch's chest and secure around the top of the skewer with edible glue. Shape the other half into a small ball for the neck, make a hole in the centre with a spare skewer and secure over the first piece with edible glue.

7 Roll 2g (pinch) of purple Sugar Dough into a sausage, flatten it and cut a 1.5cm (½") wide strip for the collar following the size guide. Cut both ends at a slight angle and attach around the top of the bodice, folding the collar over a little.

8 Roll 2g (pinch) of Green Sugar Dough into a sausage for one arm, then flatten one end between your finger and thumb to make a hand. Make four cuts in the hand to make the fingers and thumb, smooth over the edges and lengthen the fingers a little. Roll the arm out more thinly, mark on the elbow with a Dresden tool and bend it to a point. Secure the top of the arm inside the sleeve and attach the hand to the hip with edible glue.

9 Roll another Green sausage to make a second arm and hand in the same way as before. Dip the end of the 6.5cm (2½") skewer into edible glue and push it in through the end of the arm up to the hand, leaving 2cm (¾") protruding. Bend the hand downwards, spread the fingers apart and bring the forefinger and thumb together. Secure the arm in the second sleeve with edible glue and support with rolled kitchen paper as it dries. Stick the wand between the forefinger and thumb with edible glue once the arm is secure.

10 Roll 12g (just under ½oz) of Green Sugar Dough into an oval for the witch's head. Push a spare skewer into the bottom of the paste and rest the head in the palm of your hand while you work on it. Mark the mouth opening with a Dresden tool then run a bone tool underneath it to form the bottom lip. Smooth your finger over the paste to remove any grooves. Push a bone tool into the corners of the mouth to make dimples.

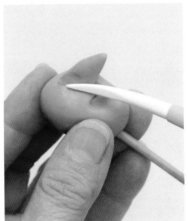

11 Shape 1g (small pinch) of Green Sugar Dough into a cone for the nose. Flatten the wider end and secure just above the mouth with edible glue. Smooth over the paste at the join with a Dresden tool. Mark on two nostrils and add lines on either side. Bend the tip of the nose downwards and mark lines for the eyes either side of the nose.

12 Pinch out two balls of Green Sugar Dough for the ears, then brush edible glue on either side of the head level with the nose. Push a bone tool into each ear to shape then attach them to either side of the head. Smooth over the paste at the front of each ear with a bone tool.

13 Roll out a small amount of Black Sugar Dough, cut out the eyelashes and attach just above the lines for the eyes. Draw on the eyebrows with a black food colour pen.

14 Shape 30g (1oz) of Red Sugar Dough into long cones of various sizes then flatten them down. Add hair lines to each section with a Dresden tool and make waves in the paste. Start attaching the hair in the centre of the back of the head, working out towards the ears. Finish attaching sections of hair over the back of the head then add strands for the fringe.

15 Roll out 6g (just under ¼oz) of Black Sugar Dough, cut out a disc with a 5cm (2") round cutter and attach to the top of the head with edible glue. Shape 15g (½oz) of Black Sugar Dough into a long cone and flatten the base on the work surface. Mark and bend the top of the hat then attach it to the middle of the disc with edible glue.

CAT

16 Make each leg from 4g (just under ¼oz) of Black Sugar Dough following the size guide. Trim the ends so they are all 5cm (2") long and attach them together in pairs. Push the 10.5cm (4¼") skewer into a spare block of polystyrene, leaving 6.5cm (2½") protruding from the top. Secure the legs around the skewer with edible glue. The feet should be level on the surface, leaving 1.5cm (½") of the skewer protruding from the top. Leave to dry.

17 Roll 12g (just under ½oz) of Black Sugar Dough into the shape of the cat's body, following the size guide. Make a hole in the underside with a spare skewer then attach over the skewered legs with edible glue.

18 Roll 2g (pinch) of Black Sugar Dough into a long cone for the tail, then cut the wider end at an angle. Attach to the back of the body with edible glue then bend the tail slightly to make kinks in it.

19 Shape 10g (¼oz) of Black Sugar Dough into a ball for the head and make a hole in the base with a small piece of dried spaghetti. Push the 2.5cm (1") piece of dried spaghetti into the front of the body, brush a little edible glue around the base then attach the head over it.

WITCH AND CAT
SIZE GUIDE

20 Mark the muzzle with the blunt edge of a knife then push the end of a drinking straw into each side at a 45° angle. Push a piece of spaghetti into the ends to make dimples. Shape a tiny ball of Black Sugar Dough into a triangle for the nose and secure in place.

21 Make two small eyeholes with the end of a paintbrush then brush a little edible glue inside each one. Secure two tiny balls of Green Sugar Dough inside the holes, then draw on the pupils with a black food colour pen.

22 Divide 1g (small pinch) of Black Sugar Dough in half and shape each piece into a triangle for the ears. Trim the bases level and wrap each one around the end of a paintbrush to shape. Attach to the top of the head with edible glue.

UNICORN

EDIBLES

SK Sugar Dough:

   130g (just over 4½oz) White

   50g (1¾oz) lilac (White +
   SK Lilac Professional Paste
   Food Colour)

   1g (small pinch) pale blue
   (White + Blue)

125g (4½oz) SK White Sugar
Florist Paste (SFP)

SK Black Professional Food
Colour Pen

SK Ice White Designer Fairy
Sparkles Dust Food Colour

SK Lilac Professional Dust
Food Colour

Important note: Remember to remove the
inedible supports before the model is eaten.

EQUIPMENT

Basic equipment (see
pages 6 to 7)

5cm (2") long wooden
barbecue skewer

3.5cm (1⅜") long strand of
dried, raw spaghetti

1 Use 30g (1oz) of White SFP for each of the back legs
and 28g (1oz) of White SFP for the front legs. Roll each
piece into a soft ball then shape into sausages for the legs.
Bend backwards at the knee and flatten each one slightly,
bending the back legs a little more than the front. Flatten the
end of each leg to make a hoof, then mark a circle around the
very base of each leg with the blunt edge of a knife. Slightly
flatten the top of each leg and leave to dry completely.

2 Shape 76g (2½oz) of White Sugar Dough into a sausage
for the body following the size guide. Pinch out a neck
from the front of the body, then insert a skewer into it as a
support for the head. Leave to dry.

3 Working on one side of the body, attach a pinch of SFP
to the top of one front and one back leg then merge
the paste onto the body with a Dresden tool. Leave to dry
completely before turning the body over and attaching the
remaining two legs. Place a piece of rolled-up kitchen towel
underneath the body to support it whilst the paste is drying.
Make sure all the legs are level when the unicorn is standing.
Once completely dry, smooth pinches of White Sugar Dough
over the joins to neaten them.

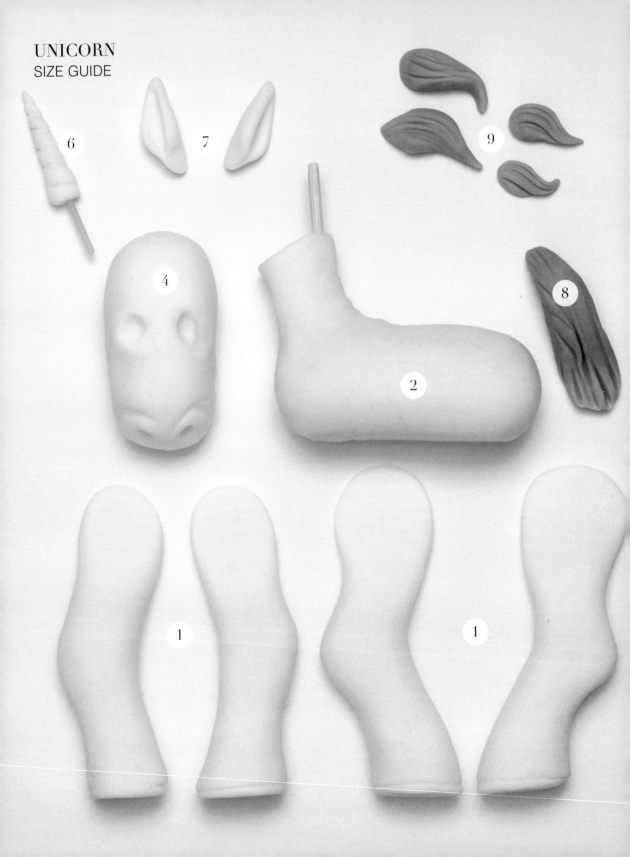

UNICORN
SIZE GUIDE

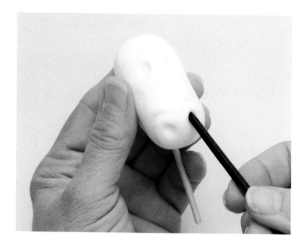
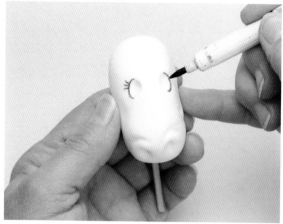

4 Shape 45g (1½oz) of White Sugar Dough into a thick
sausage for the head. Mark on the mouth with the blunt
edge of a knife and use a paintbrush handle to indent the
dimples. Make two holes for the nostrils with the end of a
paintbrush then mark around each one with a Dresden tool.
Push a bone tool into the head to create the eye sockets. Push
a spare skewer into the base of the head, remove then secure
the head over the neck with edible glue.

5 Outline the eye sockets with a black food colour pen then
draw three eyelashes on each one. Secure two small
discs of White Sugar Dough inside the eye sockets with a little
edible glue. Add two discs of pale blue Sugar Dough on top,
then add two smaller discs of Black Sugar Dough. Make a
small dent in each eye with a Dresden tool, brush with a little
edible glue and secure a tiny white highlight to each one.

6 Push the length of dried spaghetti into the head just
above and between the eyes, then remove. Shape 1g
(small pinch) of White Sugar Dough into a thin cone for the
horn. Moisten the spaghetti with edible glue then push it into
the wider end of the cone, leaving 1.5cm (½") protruding from
the end. Mark lines around the horn with a Dresden tool and
attach to the head with edible glue.

7 Shape 2g (pinch) of White Sugar Dough into a cone for
each ear, flatten them down and wrap them around a
paintbrush handle to shape. Remove and pinch the paste at
the base. Attach to either side of the head with edible glue,
bringing the ears forward slightly.

8 Shape 5g (just under ¼oz) of lilac Sugar Dough into
a cone, texture it with a Dresden tool and attach the
pointed end to the back of the body to help build up the tail.
Pinch out small balls from 8g (¼oz) of lilac Sugar Dough,
shape them into cones and flatten down. Add texture with
a Dresden tool, curl the paste a little to give it shape then
attach halfway down the first piece. Continue to cover the first
section of the tail with pieces of paste, working up towards
the unicorn's back.

9 Make the mane in the same way as the tail using 30g
(1oz) of lilac Sugar Dough, starting in the middle of
the unicorn's back
and working up
towards the ears. Use
another 6g (just under
¼oz) of lilac Sugar
Dough to add
sections of hair
either side of the
horn and between
the ears.

10 Dust the hooves, back,
neck, nostrils, inner ears
and mouth area with a mix of Lilac
and Ice White dust food colours.
Dust the remaining parts of the
unicorn just with Ice White dust
for a sparkly finish.

GNOME

EDIBLES

SK Sugar Dough:

  120g (4¼oz) Red

  45g (1½oz) Green

  40g (1½oz) White

  35g (1¼oz) Golden Bear Brown

  35g (1¼oz) Soft Beige

  15g (½oz) Blue

  1g (small pinch) Black

  1g (small pinch) Brown

  1g (small pinch) Yellow

60g (2oz) SK White Sugar Florist Paste (SFP)

SK Black Professional Food Colour Pen

EQUIPMENT

Basic equipment (see pages 6 to 7)

19cm (7½") long wooden barbecue skewer

18-gauge green floral wire

40cm (16") length of black cotton

Non-toxic craft glue

1 For the toadstool stalk, shape the White SFP into a thick sausage that is a little narrower at the top. Pinch around the top and bottom to make the ends flat, then push the 19cm (7½") long skewer through the centre so 4cm (1½") is protruding from the base. Leave to dry.

2 For the toadstool cap, roll 95g (3¼oz) of Red Sugar Dough into a ball then flatten one side on the work surface to make a dome shape, using the size guide for reference. Make a hole through the top of the dome slightly off-centre and attach a few small, white discs. Set aside.

3 Roll 20g (¾oz) of White Sugar Dough into a ball, flatten and mark lines around the edge with a Dresden tool. Push a spare skewer through the centre to make a hole. Attach to the underside of the toadstool cap with edible glue. Secure the toadstool cap over the skewered stalk and leave to dry before adding the gnome.

4 For the fishing rod, cut the green floral wire to 12.5cm (5") long and attach the length of black cotton to the wire at intervals using non-toxic glue. Wrap the cotton around the top of the rod to secure, leaving a length hanging from the end. Leave to dry.

Important note: As this figure is made using inedible supports and wires, remember to remove the model from the cake before it is served.

GNOME
SIZE GUIDE

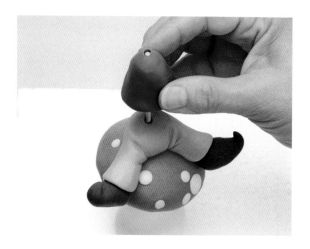

Important note: Make sure that the non-toxic glue and wire do not come into contact with any part of the cake that is going to be eaten.

5   Reserve a very small pinch of Yellow Sugar Dough and model the remaining paste into the shape of a fish, following the size guide. Mark lines over the tail with the blunt edge of a knife. Shape the reserved paste into a small fin, add lines with a knife and secure in place with edible glue. Add the eyes on either side with a black food colour pen. Make a small hole in the mouth, push the cotton fishing line into the paste and seal it over. Leave the fish to dry completely before lifting it on the rod.

6   For the gnome's legs, roll 35g (1¼oz) of Golden Bear Brown Sugar Dough into a sausage. Roll the paste either side of the centre to lengthen the legs a little whilst keeping the thickness in the middle. Mark creases at the top of the legs with a Dresden tool and make a hole through the centre with a spare skewer. Thread the legs over the skewer and secure to the top of the toadstool with edible glue.

7   Divide 15g (½oz) of Blue Sugar Dough in half for the shoes. Shape each piece into a cone and bend the pointed end up a little. Attach to the end of the trouser legs and the top of the toadstool using edible glue.

8   Shape 26g (just under 1oz) of Green Sugar Dough into a cone then push your thumb into the larger end and pinch down the paste to form a hollow in the base. Push a

spare skewer through the centre to make a hole then attach over the skewered trousers with edible glue.

9   Roll 16g (½oz) of Green Sugar Dough into a sausage with tapered ends. Cut the sausage in half to make two arms, mark the elbows with a Dresden tool and bend slightly. Push the end of a paintbrush into the wide end of each sleeve. Attach the arms to the top of the body and bring them around to the front, leaving enough room for the hands.

10   Shape 2g (pinch) of Soft Beige Sugar Dough into a cone and flatten slightly to make a hand. Make a cut in one side and bring out the thumb a little. Use a knife to make three marks for the fingers. Repeat for the second hand but cut the thumb from the opposite side. Secure inside the sleeves with edible glue, positioning one in front of the other.

11   Roll 1g (small pinch) of Soft Beige Sugar Dough into a ball for the neck. Make a hole through the centre with a spare skewer, thread over the skewered body and secure with edible glue.

12   For the head, roll 25g (just over ¾oz) of Soft Beige Sugar Dough into a ball and make a hole in the base with a spare skewer. Secure the head over the skewered neck.

13   Pinch out two small balls of Soft Beige Sugar Dough for the ears and a slightly larger one for the nose. Roll the nose into a slight oval and set aside. Brush a little

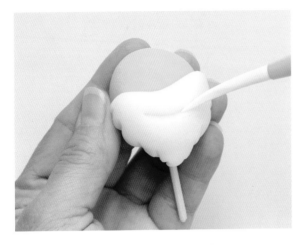

edible glue on either side of the head, then push a bone tool into each ear to shape and secure in place. Smooth over the paste at the front of each ear with a bone tool.

14 Roll 4g (just under ¼oz) of White Sugar Dough into a sausage for the hair then flatten and use a Dresden tool to add texture. Attach to the back of the head with edible glue.

15 Pinch out two small balls of White Sugar Dough and shape each into a triangle for the sideburns. Texture as before and attach in front of the ears.

16 Shape the beard from 8g (¼oz) of White Sugar Dough, following the size guide. Add texture as before then make an indent for the mouth with a Dresden tool. Attach the beard to the lower half of the face with edible glue.

17 Flatten two small balls of White Sugar Dough for the eyes and attach to the head, leaving a gap for the nose. Add two smaller discs of Brown Sugar Dough on top, then add two Black discs for the pupils. Make a small dent in each eye with a Dresden tool and attach two tiny White highlights with edible glue. Secure the nose in place.

18 Roll the remaining Black Sugar Dough into a thin sausage, cut two small lengths for the eyebrows and four small, tapered lengths for the eyelashes and attach to the face.

19 Roll 25g (just over ¾oz) of Red Sugar Dough into a cone, then push your thumb into the wider end and pinch out the paste to make it large enough to fit over the head. Secure in place, leaving space for the hair at the front.

20 Shape two small white cones for the tufts of hair, flatten them down and add texture with a Dresden tool. Secure to the front of the head, ease the hat down over them and curl the hair up over the hat.

THREE LITTLE PIGS

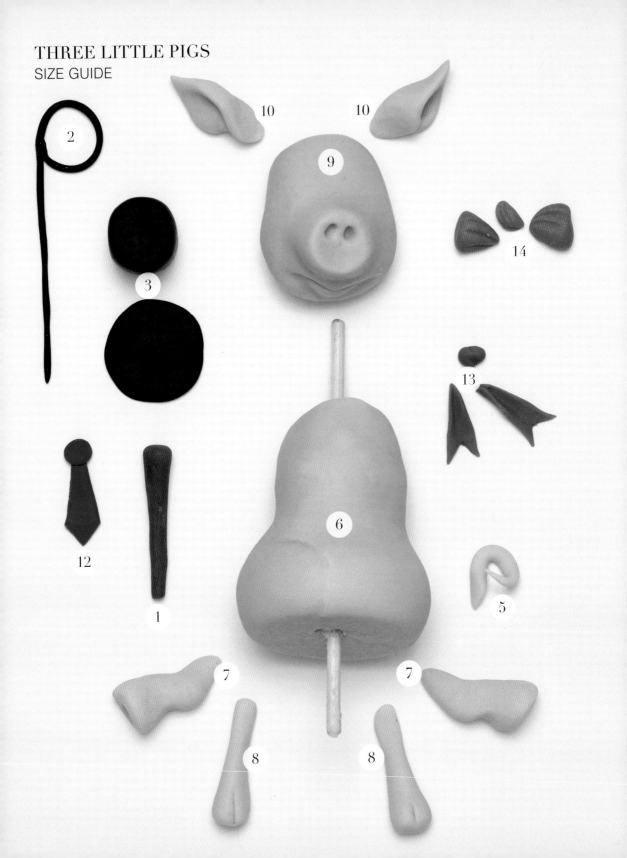

THREE LITTLE PIGS
SIZE GUIDE

EDIBLES

SK Sugar Dough:

  425g (14¾oz) Soft Beige

  15g (½oz) Black

  2g (pinch) Brown

  2g (pinch) Green

  2g (pinch) Red

  1g (small pinch) Blue

  1g (small pinch) White

SK Black Professional Food Colour Pen

SK Pastel Pink Designer Dust Food Colour

EQUIPMENT

Basic equipment (see pages 6 to 7)

2 x 12.5cm and 1 x 14cm and (2 x 5" and 1 x 5½") long wooden barbecue skewers

3.5cm (1⅜") long strand of dried, raw spaghetti

1 To make the walking stick, roll 2g (pinch) of Brown Sugar Dough into a sausage, dip a 3.5cm (1⅜") strand of dried spaghetti into edible glue and push it all the way into the sausage. Make the paste thicker at the top of the stick, add texture with a Dresden tool and set aside.

2 For the monocle, roll 1g (small pinch) of Black Sugar Dough into a thin sausage then bend one end around to form a circle. Set aside.

3 To make the top hat, roll 2g (small pinch) of Black Sugar Dough into a ball then flatten it into a disc. Shape 8g (¼oz) into a cylinder and attach on top of the disc with edible glue. Set aside.

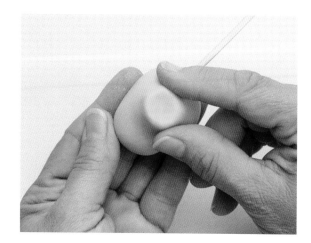

Important note: Remember to remove the barbecue skewers and inedible parts before the models are eaten.

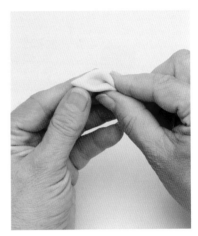

4   Divide the Soft Beige Sugar Dough into three equal pieces for the three pigs then divide each piece as follows: 100g (3½oz) for the body, 6g (just under ¼oz) for the back legs, 8g (¼oz) for the front legs, 25g (just over ¾oz) for the head and 2g (small pinch) for the ears. Make the parts for each of the three pigs at the same time.

5   Pinch out a small ball of Soft Beige Sugar Dough from the 100g (3½oz) for each body, roll it into a small sausage and curl it around to make a small tail.

6   Model the rest of the Soft Beige Sugar Dough for each body into a pear shape. Push a 14cm (5½") skewer down through the centre of the body for the pig with a top hat, then do the same with the 12.5cm (5") skewers for the other two pigs. Attach a tail to the back of each body with edible glue.

7   For the back legs, roll 3g (⅛oz) of Soft Beige Sugar Dough per leg into a short, thick sausage. Flatten one end to make a trotter shape then narrow the paste at the ankle. Bend the paste to make the knee and flatten the top a little. Brush edible glue on either side of the body, attach the top of each leg to the body and smooth over the join with a Dresden tool. Mark the hips on either side of the body with a Dresden tool. Push the end of a bone tool into the base of each trotter and mark across the top with the blunt edge of a knife.

8   For the front legs, roll 4g (just under ¼oz) of Soft Beige Sugar Dough per leg into a sausage that tapers a little at the top. Mark the front of the trotters with the blunt edge of a knife and attach to the front of the body with edible glue. Smooth the paste onto the body with a Dresden tool. For one pig with a 12.5cm (5") skewer through its body, lift one leg up onto the walking stick and secure to the top with edible glue.

9   To make each head, roll 25g (just over ¾oz) of Soft Beige Sugar Dough into a ball then push a spare skewer into the base and rest it in the palm of your hand while you work on it. Carefully ease out the paste at the front with your fingers to form a snout and mark the mouth underneath with a Dresden tool. Run a bone tool underneath the mouth to form a bottom lip then smooth over any grooves in the paste with your finger. Push a bone tool into the corners of the mouth to make dimples. Use the end of a paintbrush to make eye sockets and nostrils. Remove the skewer then attach the head to the body with edible glue.

10   Roll 1g (small pinch) of Soft Beige Sugar Dough into a cone for each ear, flatten it down and wrap it around a paintbrush handle to shape. Pinch the ends and attach to the side of the head with edible glue. Push the end of a bone tool inside each ear to open it up a little.

11   Brush a tiny amount of edible glue inside the eye sockets and secure a tiny ball of Black Sugar

Dough in each one. Make a small dent in each eye with a Dresden tool, brush with a little edible glue and add tiny highlights made from White Sugar Dough. Draw on the eyebrows with a black food colour pen.

12 For the pig with the longer skewer through its body, roll out the Blue Sugar Dough and cut out the tie shape following the size guide. Attach just under the chin with edible glue. Make a small ball from the trimmings and attach to the top of the tie with edible glue. Secure the top hat to its head with edible glue.

13 For the pig with the walking stick, roll out the Green Sugar Dough and cut out two strips for the neck tie following the size guide. Pinch the paste together at the top and attach both pieces just under the head with edible glue. Roll the remaining green paste into a ball, attach to the top of the strips and add creases with a Dresden tool.

14 For the third pig, pinch out a small ball from 2g (pinch) of Red Sugar Dough then divide the remaining paste in half. Shape the two halves into triangles for the bowtie, add creases with a Dresden tool and secure just under the head with edible glue. Roll the small ball into a sausage, attach over the ends of the triangles and add creases with a Dresden tool. Attach the monocle just below the pig's eye, resting the handle on the side of its head.

15 Dust the pigs' cheeks with Pastel Pink dust food colour to finish.

INCY WINCY SPIDER

EDIBLES

SK Sugar Dough:

  150g (5¼oz) Black

  2g (pinch) White

  1g (small pinch) Green

EQUIPMENT

Basic equipment (see pages 6 to 7)

18-gauge floral wires: 4 x green

Half-width white floral tape

6cm (2⅜") polystyrene ball

1 Bend all four wires into shape for the legs following the size guide. Arrange the wires so that they all overlap at a central point then firmly secure with floral tape.

2 Wrap a 10g (¼oz) sausage of Black Sugar Dough around each of the legs, using edible glue to secure the paste down each wire. Work in opposite pairs to keep the spider balanced and leave each pair to dry before moving onto the next one. Support the legs with rolled kitchen paper whilst they dry.

Important note: As this figure is made using inedible supports, remember to remove the spider from the cake before it is served.

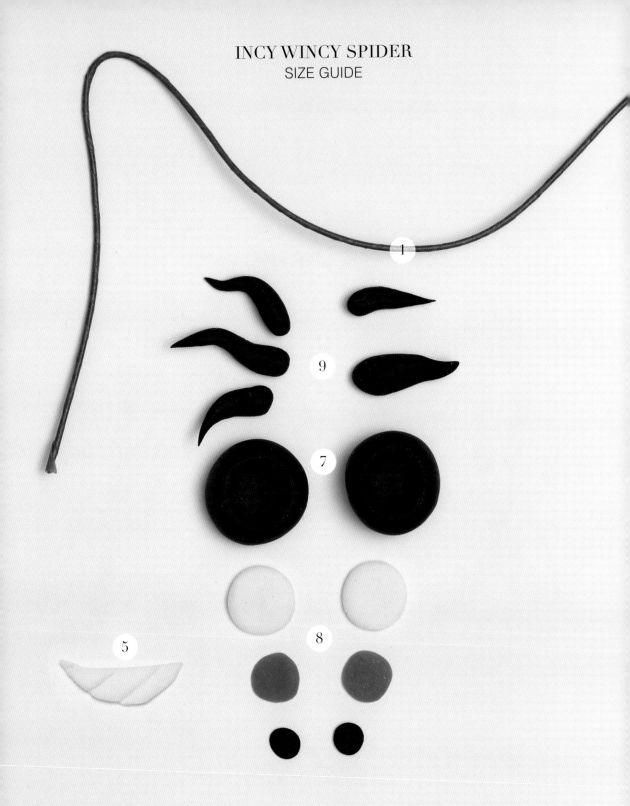

3   Roll 2g (pinch) of Black Sugar Dough into a ball, flatten it into a disc and attach underneath the central point where the legs overlap. Secure with edible glue.

4   Push a spare skewer into the base of the polystyrene ball so that you can hold this while covering the ball. Roll out 35g (1¼oz) of Black Sugar Dough, dampen the ball with a little cooled, boiled water and cover with the paste. Smooth over the paste until the ball is completely covered.

5   Mark the mouth opening at the front of the ball with a Dresden tool. Open the mouth a little to make the lips at the top and bottom, then mark the corner of the mouth with a Dresden tool. Roll out 1g (small pinch) of White Sugar Dough and cut a piece to fit inside the mouth opening, following the size guide. Make indents for the teeth with a small knife and secure inside the opening with edible glue. Ease the top and bottom lips over the teeth slightly.

6   Remove the skewer from the base of the body. Roll out a small disc from 2g (pinch) of Black Sugar Dough and secure over the top of the central join in the legs. Attach the body to the top of the disc and the legs with edible glue.

7   Roll two 5g (just under ¼oz) balls of Black Sugar Dough for the eyes and attach to the top of the head with edible glue.

8   Divide 1g (small pinch) of White Sugar Dough in half and make two discs to fit onto the black eyeballs. Add two green discs on top, then two smaller black discs for the pupils. Push the Dresden tool into the eyes and add tiny pieces of paste for the highlights.

9   Pinch out small pieces of paste from 20g (¾oz) of Black Sugar Dough, shape them into cones for the hair and attach to the top of the head and eyes with edible glue. Attach some around the back of the eyes, shaping each one as you go.

PIRATE AND PARROT

EDIBLES

SK Sugar Dough:

130g (just over 4½oz) Blue

35g (just over 1¼oz) Soft Beige

30g (1oz) Black

25g (just over ¾oz) White

15g (½oz) Golden Bear Brown

15g (½oz) Brown

10g (¼oz) Yellow

8g (¼oz) grey (White + Black)

5g (just under ¼oz) Red

5g (just under ¼oz) Green

2g (small pinch) Orange

SK Black Professional Food Colour Pen

Important note: As this figure is made using inedible supports, remember to remove the model from the cake before it is served.

EQUIPMENT

Basic equipment (see pages 6 to 7)

6cm (2⅜") polystyrene ball

23cm (9") long wooden barbecue skewer

4cm (1½") long strand of dried, raw spaghetti

PIRATE

1 For the boot, reserve a small ball from 15g (½oz) of Black Sugar Dough then roll the rest into a sausage. Cut 2cm (¾") off one end and set this piece aside. Place your finger on top of the rounded end and gently lift up the other end to form a boot shape. Pinch the 2cm (¾") piece between your finger and thumb to make a small hollow in the base. Attach to the top of the boot with edible glue.

2 Roll out the reserved ball of Black Sugar Dough and cut out a small square. Roll out 1g (small pinch) of Yellow Sugar Dough, stick the black square on top with edible glue and cut out a larger rectangle for the buckle. Attach to the top of the boot with a little edible glue, then set the boot aside.

3 To make the peg leg, roll 5g (just under ¼oz) of Golden Bear Brown Sugar Dough into a sausage. Cut each end straight and add a woodgrain texture with a Dresden tool. Roll 3g (⅛oz) of Golden Bear Brown Sugar Dough into a ball, flatten it slightly between your finger and thumb then attach it to the top of the sausage with edible glue. The peg leg should be shorter than the boot, so trim down if necessary then set aside.

PIRATE
AND
PARROT
SIZE GUIDE

4 Roll 12g (just under ½oz) of Blue Sugar Dough into a sausage for the trousers. Cut the Sugar Dough in two, making one leg slightly longer than the other. Set aside.

5 Push the wooden barbecue skewer into the centre of the polystyrene ball so it is slightly off-centre – this will support the leg with the boot. Brush a little edible glue over the surface then roll out 30g (1oz) of Blue Sugar Dough and cover the ball completely, joining the paste together at the top. Cut away any excess and smooth the surface with a cake smoother.

6 Push the skewer from the body into the top of the shorter leg and down into the boot, leaving 5cm (2") protruding from the base. Secure the pieces together with edible glue, leaving a little gap between the ball and the top of the trousers.

7 Attach the other trouser leg to the peg leg with edible glue. Shape 1g (small pinch) of Blue Sugar Dough into a disc, attach it to the top of the peg leg and secure to the polystyrene ball. Add creases with a Dresden tool. Roll out a 1g (small pinch) sausage of Blue Sugar Dough to fill in the gap at the top of the skewered leg. Attach it around the leg with edible glue, mark creases and leave to dry.

8 For the shirt, shape 20g (¾oz) of White Sugar Dough into a cone, push your thumb into the wider end and pinch the Sugar Dough out to form a hollow so it will sit comfortably over the polystyrene ball. Make a hole slightly off-centre through the cone with a spare skewer and secure over the skewered body with edible glue.

9 For the lower half of the jacket, roll out 30g (1oz) of Blue Sugar Dough and cut a long strip to fit around the body. Attach around the base of the shirt and mark creases across the top with a Dresden tool. Lift out the bottom of the jacket in a couple of places to add movement. Shape 30g (1oz) of Blue Sugar Dough into a cone and pinch out a hollow in the same way as for the shirt. Fit it over the white shirt and secure in place with edible glue.

10 Shape 1g (small pinch) of Soft Beige Sugar Dough into a disc, make a hole through the centre with a spare skewer then attach over the skewered body with edible glue to form the neck.

11 Roll 4g (just under ¼oz) of Golden Bear Brown Sugar Dough into a sausage, flatten it and cut out a 5mm (¼") wide strip. Cut and reserve a square from one end, then secure the strip around the join in the jacket with edible glue. Roll out 1g (small pinch) of Yellow Sugar Dough, stick the Golden Bear Brown square in the centre and cut out a larger rectangle for the belt buckle. Secure in place with edible glue.

12 Use 2g (pinch) of Yellow Sugar Dough to make the buttons and braid. Roll 10 small balls for the buttons and set aside. Roll the remaining paste into a thin sausage and cut it into five equal sections, then cut one of these pieces in half. Stick four lengths of braiding above the belt and the two short pieces below it. Brush a little edible glue on the ends of the strips, push the end of a paintbrush into the centre of each button and secure to the jacket.

13 For the arms, roll 20g (¾oz) of Blue Sugar Dough into a sausage with tapered ends, cut it in half and mark creases at the elbows with a Dresden tool. Make a hole in the wide end of the sleeves with a paintbrush handle then bend slightly at the elbow. Attach the arms to the sides of the body, positioning one at the front just under the belt and the other behind the body.

14 Roll out 2g (pinch) of Blue Sugar Dough for the collar and cut out a strip to fit around the neck. Secure to the neck with the opening at the front.

15 Shape 1g (small pinch) of Blue Sugar Dough into two cones for the epaulettes, flatten slightly and round off the ends. Secure to the shoulders with edible glue.

16 For the hook, divide 3g (⅛oz) of Grey Sugar Dough into two equal pieces. Roll one piece into a ball and pinch the end into a point to fit inside the sleeve, then push the end of a paintbrush into the centre to accommodate the hook. Shape the second piece into a long, pointed cone, bend the pointed end into a hook and pinch the wider end into a point to fit inside the first piece. Secure the pieces together with edible glue and attach inside the sleeve, holding in place until secure.

17 For the cutlass, roll out 3g (⅛oz) of grey Sugar Dough and cut out a blade shape following the size guide. Mark a ridge along the side with a Dresden tool and pinch the end into a small handle. Shape 1g (small pinch) of Brown Sugar Dough into a sausage, push the end of a paintbrush into one end and secure the blade inside it with edible glue. For the hand guard, roll out 2g (pinch) of grey Sugar Dough, cut out a small strip following the size guide and round off both ends. Roll a small grey ball from the trimmings, then set the pieces of the cutlass aside.

18 Shape 3g (⅛oz) of Soft Beige Sugar Dough into a cone for the hand, flatten it slightly and make a cut in one side for the thumb. Ease out the paste a little and smooth over the edge. Use a knife to make three marks for the fingers then indent the top of the fingers with a Dresden tool.

19 Brush edible glue inside the hand and secure the cutlass in place, wrapping the fingers around the handle slightly. Brush edible glue inside the sleeve and attach the hand, holding until it is completely secure. Attach the guard over the hand and stick the small ball on top.

20 Pinch out a small ball from 25g (just over ¾oz) of Soft Beige Sugar Dough for the nose and set aside. Shape the remaining paste into a ball for the head, push a spare skewer into the base and rest it in the palm of your hand. Mark the mouth opening with a Dresden tool then run a bone tool underneath to form a bottom lip.

21 Attach the nose above the mouth then smooth the paste onto the face with a Dresden tool. Pinch up the bridge of the nose then add nostrils with the end of a paintbrush. Mark the sides of the nose with a Dresden tool and make a small indent for the eye with a bone tool. Remove the skewer and attach the head over the skewered neck with edible glue.

22 Brush edible glue on either side of the head level with the nose, then divide 1g (small pinch) of Soft Beige Sugar Dough in half for the ears. Roll each piece into a ball then push a bone tool into each ear and attach to the side of the head. Smooth over the paste at the front of the ears with a bone tool.

23 Divide 1g (small pinch) of Black Sugar Dough in half and roll one half into a thin sausage for the moustache. Attach to the underside of the nose with edible glue and curl the ends back on themselves. Shape the second piece into a long triangle for the beard, add texture with a Dresden tool and attach to the chin with edible glue.

24 Secure a small ball of White Sugar Dough in the eye socket, then attach a very small disc of Brown Sugar Dough on top. Add a smaller black disc for the pupil. Make a small dent in each eye with a Dresden tool, brush with a little edible glue and add a tiny piece of white paste for the highlight.

25 Shape a small ball of Soft Beige Sugar Dough into a slim cone following the size guide and attach above the eye. Roll a small ball of Black Sugar Dough into a sausage and attach over the brow with edible glue.

26 For the eyepatch, shape 1g (small pinch) of Black Sugar Dough into an oval and flatten it down. Cut to size and attach to the head with edible glue. Roll the trimmings into a thin sausage for the strap and attach across the top of the head at an angle.

27 Divide 12g (just under ½oz) of Brown Sugar Dough into 6g (just under ¼oz) for the hair at the back of the head, 1g (small pinch) for the tip of the ponytail and 5g (just under ¼oz) for the curls. Model the paste for the back of the head into a triangular shape, add texture with a Dresden tool and secure to the head and top of the jacket. Smooth a little of the paste onto the head. Shape the tip of the ponytail into a cone, add texture with a Dresden tool and attach to the base of the hair.

28 For the bow, reserve a tiny ball from 1g (small pinch) of Red Sugar Dough then divide the rest into two small triangles. Attach them between the pieces of hair, mark with a Dresden tool then secure the ball between the triangles.

29 Pinch out a few small pieces of Brown Sugar Dough at a time, shape them into long cones and twist them into curls. Secure curls around the ears with edible glue.

30 Roll 10g (¼oz) of Black Sugar Dough into a ball, push your thumb into the underside and pinch out the paste to open the base of the hat. Slightly flatten the paste to make sure it covers the top of the head and secure in place. Roll out 2g (pinch) of Black Sugar Dough and cut two strips to fit either side of the hat. Cut the ends at an angle and secure to the hat with edible glue.

31 Roll out 1g (pinch) of White Sugar Dough and cut out a skull and crossbones design with a sharp knife, following the size guide. Attach to the front of the hat with edible glue.

PARROT

32 Shape 1g (small pinch) of Red Sugar Dough into a cone for the body, push the piece of spaghetti down the centre and mark wings on either side with a Dresden tool. Set aside.

33 For the tail, pinch out two unequal pieces of Yellow, Red and Green Sugar Dough and 1g (small pinch) of Orange Sugar Dough. Shape each piece into long cones and attach the thinner ends to the top of the pirate's shoulder with edible glue. Rest the wider ends over the back of the arm and secure in place with edible glue.

34 Push the parrot's body into the top of the pirate's shoulder over the tail pieces and secure with a little edible glue.

35 Shape a small ball of Orange Sugar Dough into a disc for the parrot's head. Push a spare piece of spaghetti into the base of the head, rest it in your palm and draw on the eyes with a black food colour pen. Remove the spare spaghetti and secure over the body with a little edible glue. Shape a tiny amount of Yellow Sugar Dough into a triangle, bend one end downward and attach to the front of the head.

36 Make small cones from Red, Yellow, Green and Orange Sugar Dough. Attach them to the parrot's head, working forwards from the back of the head with the cones flopping over slightly.

MERMAID

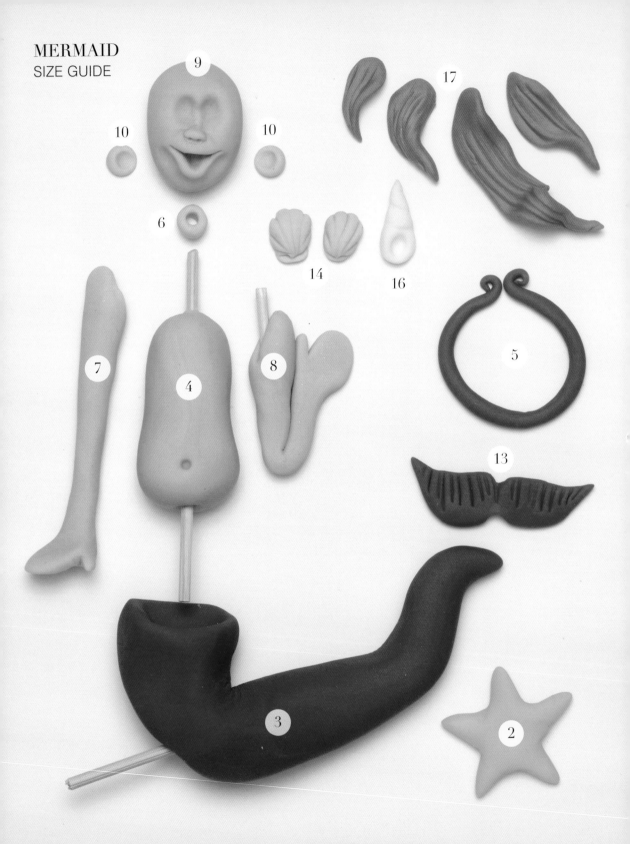

MERMAID
SIZE GUIDE

EDIBLES

SK Sugar Dough:

   120g (4¼oz) Golden Bear Brown

   100g (3½oz) Orange

   70g (2½oz) Green

   50g (1¾oz) Soft Beige

   4g (just under ¼oz) Yellow

   2g (pinch) pink (White + Red)

   2g (pinch) White

   1g (small pinch) pale blue (White + Blue)

   1g (small pinch) Black

SK Fern Professional Dust Food Colour

SK Professional Food Colour Pens: Black and Red

SK Ice White Designer Fairy Sparkles Dust Food Colour

Important note: Remember to remove the barbecue skewers before the model is eaten.

EQUIPMENT

Basic equipment (see pages 6 to 7)

12.5cm (5") round cake card

7cm, 9cm and 10cm (2¾", 3½" and 4") long wooden barbecue skewers

1 Dampen the cake card with a little cooled, boiled water. Place the Golden Bear Brown Sugar Dough in the centre of the cake card, then roll out the paste around the edges to cover the card whilst keeping a mound of paste in the middle. Trim any excess paste from around the edge of the card with a knife then texture the surface with the end of a paintbrush and a bone tool.

2 Shape 4g (just under ¼oz) of Yellow Sugar Dough into a disc and pinch out five points to make a star shape. Attach the starfish to the cake card with edible glue and texture with a Dresden tool.

3 For the tail, shape 65g (2¼oz) of Green Sugar Dough into a sausage that tapers at one end. Push your thumb into the larger end and gently pinch out the paste to form a hollow for the body to fit inside. Bend the tail slightly then push a 10cm (4") skewer into the side and along the length of the tail for support. Push the skewer into the mound on the cake card, secure with edible glue and support with rolled kitchen paper as it dries. Bend the end of the tail so it points upwards.

4 Shape 22g (just over ¾oz) of Soft Beige Sugar Dough into a thick sausage for the torso, making it a little narrower at one end. Check that the wider end fits inside the hollow in the top of the tail. Push the 9cm (3½") skewer down into the body with a twisting motion, brush edible glue in the hollow then push the skewer through the tail and into the mound on the cake card. Support with more rolled kitchen paper if necessary.

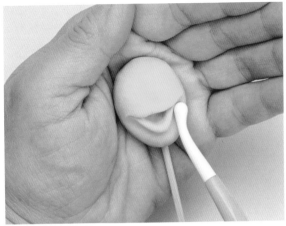

5 Roll a long, thin sausage with tapered ends from 3g (¹⁄₈oz) of Green Sugar Dough. Brush a little edible glue around the join between the body and tail and secure the band in place, curling the ends back on themselves.

6 For the neck, roll a small ball of Soft Beige Sugar Dough, gently squeeze it between your finger and thumb then push a spare skewer through the centre to make a ring. Attach to the top of the skewered body with edible glue and leave to dry.

7 For the straight arm, roll 6g (just under ¹⁄₄oz) of Soft Beige Sugar Dough into a sausage and cut one end at an angle to fit against the body. Pinch the other end between your finger and thumb to make a hand, then make a cut in one side and ease out the paste to make the thumb. Remove the kitchen paper supports and attach the arm to the side of the body with edible glue. Smooth over the join at the shoulder with a Dresden tool.

8 Make the second arm in the same way, but this time insert a skewer into the shoulder and halfway down the arm with a twisting motion. Push a spare skewer into the side of the body to make a hole then secure the skewered arm into it with edible glue. Mark the elbow with a Dresden tool and bend the arm back on itself. Smooth over the join at the shoulder then rest the hand over it, supporting the arm with rolled kitchen paper until dry.

9 Take 12g (just under ¹⁄₂oz) of Soft Beige Sugar Dough for the head, then pinch out two small balls for the ears and

reserve. Shape the remaining paste into an oval, push a spare skewer into the base and rest the head in the palm of your hand while you work on it. Mark on the mouth with a Dresden tool then turn the end of the tool upwards to lift the paste and form a top lip. Turn the tool downwards to open up the bottom of the mouth. Use a Dresden tool to mark the corners, then run a bone tool under the bottom lip to push it out. Smooth over the paste with your finger then push a bone tool into the corners to lift the cheeks and give her a smile.

10 Use a ball tool to gently push out the paste in the middle of the face and bring out a small nose. Push the handle of a paintbrush into the end of the nose to make nostrils. Make two small indents for the eyes with a bone tool. Mark smile lines either side of the nose with a Dresden tool. Push a bone tool into each ear and secure to either side of the head. Remove the skewer and secure over the neck with edible glue.

11 Outline the eye sockets with a black food colour pen, draw three eyelashes on each eye and add eyebrows. Secure a disc of White Sugar Dough inside each eye socket with edible glue. Attach two very small discs of pale blue Sugar Dough on top, then add two smaller black discs for the pupils. Make a small dent in each eye with a Dresden tool, brush with a little edible glue and add tiny white highlights.

12 Brush a little edible glue inside the mouth and add a small piece of Black Sugar Dough, smoothing it into the back of the mouth with a Dresden tool. Draw over the lips

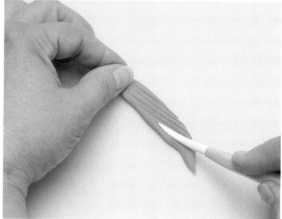

with a red food colour pen then soften the colour with a damp paintbrush. Leave the head to firm slightly before attaching the hair.

13 Shape 3g (¹/₈oz) of Green Sugar Dough into the fin for the end of the tail, following the size guide. Mark the surface with the blunt edge of a knife, bring the ends to a point and secure to the end of the tail with edible glue. If necessary, support with a small piece of kitchen paper until dry.

14 Roll 1g (small pinch) of pink Sugar Dough into a ball for each of the pink shells. Flatten slightly then mark the surface with the blunt edge of a knife. Straighten the base with the side of a knife. Use edible glue to attach both shells to the top of the body.

15 Brush a small line of edible glue across the neck just above the shells. Roll tiny balls of White Sugar Dough for the pearls and arrange them around the neck, working from the back to the front.

16 Shape 1g (small pinch) of White Sugar Dough into a cone for the conch shell. Mark lines over the surface with a Dresden tool, starting at the tip and working around the shell. Push the end of a bone tool into the larger end then secure to the hand with edible glue.

17 Brush the mermaid's head with edible glue to make it sticky before attaching the hair. Roll small pieces of Orange Sugar Dough into long cone shapes, run a Dresden tool down the paste several times and attach to the head, working from the back of the head out towards the ears. Add smaller sections of hair around the front of the face and on top of the head.

18 Mix some Ice White sparkle dust with a little Fern dust food colour and brush the colour over the tail. Brush Ice White sparkle dust over the shells and the starfish to finish.

OGRE

EDIBLES

150g (5¼oz) marshmallow
rice cereal mix (see recipe on
page 10)
60g (2oz) SK White Sugar
Florist Paste (SFP)
SK Sugar Dough:
   230g (8¼oz) Soft Beige
   120g (4¼oz) light brown
   (110g (3¾oz) White + 10g
   (¼oz) Brown)
   100g (3½oz) Brown
   15g (½oz) Black
   8g (¼oz) White
   1g (small pinch) Yellow
SK Professional Food Colour
Pens: Brown and Red
SK Bulrush Professional Dust
Food Colour

Important note: Remember to remove the
inedible supports before the model is eaten.

EQUIPMENT

Basic equipment (see
pages 6 to 7)
17.5cm (7") long wooden
barbecue skewer
4cm (1½") long strand of
dried, raw spaghetti

1 Model the marshmallow rice cereal mix into the shape
of the ogre's body following the size guide and leave to
cool completely (see page 10).

2 Shape the legs from White SFP following the size guide.
Push the barbecue skewer up through the centre of the
legs and into the body, leaving 5cm (2") protruding from the
base. Mark a seam down the front and back of the legs with a
Dresden tool and leave to dry completely.

3 For the pipe, take 1g (small pinch) of Brown Sugar
Dough and reserve a small amount for the bowl. Dip
the spaghetti in edible glue then carefully ease the remaining
paste along it, leaving 1.5cm (½") uncovered. Shape the
reserved Brown Sugar Dough into a ball, push the end of a
bone tool into the centre to make a bowl shape and attach to
the covered end of the spaghetti piece with edible glue. Set
aside to dry.

4 To make the trousers, roll out the light brown Sugar
Dough and cover the lower half of the body and legs.
Use a knife to cut the edges straight at the top and bottom,
then reserve the trimmings for the belt loops. Smooth over the
paste with a cake smoother then add creases at the top of the
legs with a Dresden tool.

5 Take 40g (1½oz) of Brown Sugar Dough for each shoe and shape following the size guide. Fit them around the bottom of the legs then run the blunt side of a knife around the base of each shoe to make the soles. Make the holes for the laces with a paintbrush handle then secure the shoes to the legs with edible glue. Use a Dresden tool to make a couple of rough holes in the top of each shoe.

6 Roll out 10g (¼oz) of Brown Sugar Dough and cut out a rectangle to form the back of the shoes. Mark a line for the sole and attach around the back of the legs with edible glue. Mark a line with the blunt edge of a knife to separate the backs of the shoes. Fill the holes at the front of the shoes with small amounts of Black Sugar Dough.

7 Roll 2g (pinch) of Brown Sugar Dough into a long, thin sausage and cut it into eight sections for the laces. Secure two pieces between the lace holes in each shoe, then attach two loose pieces either side to make the ends of the laces.

8 Draw vertical stripes around the trousers using a brown food colour pen.

9 For the belt, roll out 8g (¼oz) of Brown Sugar Dough into a thin sausage then flatten it down. Cut out a long strip to fit around the circumference of the body with a little overhang at the end. Cut a square off the end and reserve it for the buckle. Attach the belt around the trousers with edible glue, starting from the front.

10 Roll out 1g (small pinch) of Black Sugar Dough, stick the reserved Brown square in the centre and cut a slightly larger square for the belt buckle. Attach to the front of the belt with edible glue. Roll a tiny sausage of Black Sugar Dough and attach inside the buckle.

11 Roll out the remaining light brown Sugar Dough and cut out nine small rectangles for the belt loops. Secure in place at equal intervals around the belt and smooth the paste onto the trousers with a Dresden tool.

12 Roll out 40g (1½oz) of Soft Beige Sugar Dough and cover the upper half of the marshmallow rice cereal body, leaving the head uncovered. Smooth over any bumps

with a cake smoother, mark on the belly button with the end of a paintbrush and add a few wrinkles with a Dresden tool.

13 For each arm, shape 45g (1½oz) of Soft Beige Sugar Dough into a sausage and flatten one end slightly to make a hand. Use a small knife to make three cuts for the fingers then smooth over the paste. Mark the fingers and wrist with a Dresden tool. Pinch and shape the paste at the other end of the arm then mark the elbows with a Dresden tool. Bend each arm and attach around the sides of the body with edible glue. Push a bone tool into the end of each finger for the nails. Smooth the shoulders onto the body with a Dresden tool and add more creases over the arms.

14 Shape 8g (¼oz) of Soft Beige Sugar Dough into a wedge to form the back of the neck and secure in place. Add a few wrinkles with a Dresden tool then smooth the paste onto the body.

15 Roll out 60g (2oz) of Soft Beige Sugar Dough and cover the head completely. Tuck the Sugar Dough underneath the chin and neck then use a Dresden tool to add creases.

16 Open up the mouth slightly with a Dresden tool. Shape 4g (just under ¼oz) of Soft Beige Sugar Dough into an oval shape for the top lip and add wrinkles with the Dresden tool. Attach it above the mouth with edible glue then blend the paste onto the head.

17 For the fangs, roll four small balls from 2g (pinch) of White Sugar Dough, leaving a small amount for the other teeth. Shape the fangs into points following the size guide then attach two fangs to the bottom lip and two under the top lip. Roll out the remaining White Sugar Dough and cut out two small rectangles of slightly different sizes, then mark a line down one piece to make two teeth. Attach both pieces inside the bottom lip with edible glue.

18 Shape 10g (¼oz) of Soft Beige Sugar Dough into an oval for the nose and attach above the mouth. Smooth the Sugar Dough onto the head with a Dresden tool and use a bone tool to indent the nostrils. Mark around the sides of the nose with a Dresden tool then continue to add wrinkles over the cheeks.

19 Roll two 3g (1/8oz) balls of Soft Beige Sugar Dough for the ears and push a bone tool into each one to hollow it out. Brush a little edible glue on either side of the head and attach the ears. Smooth the paste at the front of each ear onto the head.

20 Run a Dresden tool across the back of the head several times to make more wrinkles.

21 Make a small hole in the front and back of one ear lobe with a Dresden tool. Roll out a thin sausage of Yellow Sugar Dough, brush a little edible glue in the holes and attach the paste to make an earring.

22 Roll one 3g (1/8oz) and one 2g (pinch) ball of White Sugar Dough for the eyes, make a dent in each one with a bone tool then attach them to the top of the head with edible glue. Attach a small disc of Brown Sugar Dough to each eyeball, then add two smaller black discs for the pupils. Make a small dent in each eye with a Dresden tool, brush with a little edible glue and add tiny white highlights. Draw on veins with a red food colour pen.

23 Shape the lower lids using 1g (small pinch) of Soft Beige Sugar Dough for each one, mark with a Dresden tool and attach with edible glue. Smooth the ends of the paste onto the face with a Dresden tool.

24 Shape one upper eyelid from 3g (1/8oz) and one from 4g (just under 1/4oz) of Soft Beige Sugar Dough

following the size guide. Secure over the eyeballs and add creases either side of the lids.

25 Push the end of a paintbrush into the nose, cheek and chin to make holes for the warts. Pinch out small pieces of Brown Sugar Dough and secure them in the holes with edible glue.

26 For the hair, make several different-sized cones from 10g (1/4oz) of Black Sugar Dough. Attach a few to the chin, nostrils, elbows, ears and eyelids then secure the rest to the back of the head. Secure each piece in place with a Dresden tool and edible glue.

27 Secure the pipe to the corner of the mouth with edible glue.

28 Brush the body lightly with Bulrush dust food colour, using more dust in the creases and wrinkles to add depth.

OGRE SIZE GUIDE

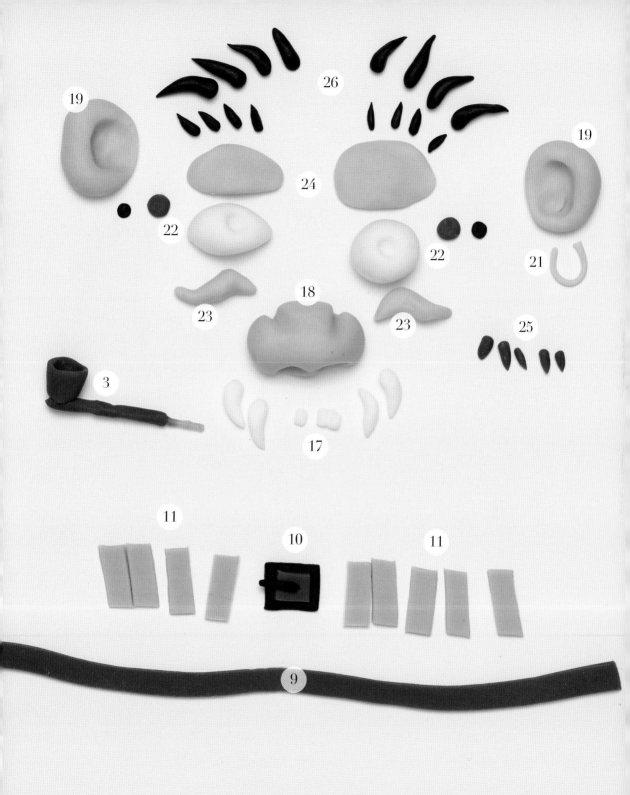

LITTLE RED RIDING HOOD

EDIBLES

SK Sugar Dough:

  140g (5oz) Red

  20g (¾oz) Golden Bear
  Brown

  15g (½oz) Soft Beige

  2g (pinch) White

  1g (small pinch) pale blue
  (White + Blue)

EQUIPMENT

Basic equipment (see
pages 6 to 7)

2.5cm and 16.5cm (1" and
6½") long wooden barbecue
skewers

1 Shape 65g (2¼oz) of Red Sugar Dough into a rounded
   cone following the size guide. Push the 16.5cm (6½")
long skewer down through the centre, leaving 5cm (2")
protruding from the base. Use a Dresden tool to mark a
waistline around the cone approximately 2.5cm (1") from the
top. Run the Dresden tool up and down the skirt section to
make pleats in the dress. Leave to dry.

2 Shape 3g (⅛oz) of Golden Bear Brown Sugar Dough
   into a cube and push the end of a bone tool into the top

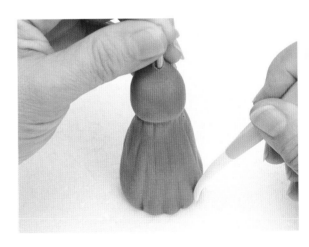

Important note: Remember to remove the
barbecue skewers before the model is eaten.

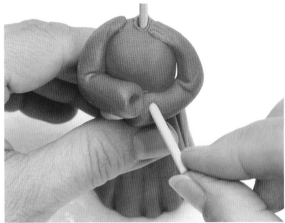

to hollow out the basket. Mark six horizontal lines around the outside of the basket with a Dresden tool.

3 Roll out 1g (small pinch) of White Sugar Dough and cut out a 2.5cm (1") square with a sharp knife. Give the cloth a little pinch in the centre and stick it to the top of the basket so it overhangs the rim.

4 Roll a small sausage of Golden Bear Brown Sugar Dough for the handle and attach it to either side of the basket with edible glue. Press a paintbrush handle into the ends to secure them in place. Push the 2.5cm (1") long skewer into one side to make a hole, then set the basket aside to dry.

5 Roll 8g (¼oz) of Red Sugar Dough into a sausage with tapered ends. Cut the sausage in half to make two arms, then push the end of a paintbrush into the wider end of each sleeve. Mark the elbows with a Dresden tool and bend slightly. Use edible glue to attach the first arm to the shoulder and across the body. Attach the second arm in the same way but lift it over the top of the first arm and secure with edible glue.

6 Brush a little edible glue over the end of the lower arm and use a bone tool to push a small ball of Soft Beige Sugar Dough into it. Shape 1g (small pinch) of Soft Beige Sugar Dough into a cone and flatten it to make a hand. Make a cut in one side to bring out the thumb, then set aside.

7 Mark where the basket will sit comfortably then push a 2.5cm (1") skewer into the arm or body, leaving enough protruding to support the basket.

8 Roll a small ball of Soft Beige Sugar Dough for the neck and make a hole in the centre with a spare skewer. Attach to the top of the skewered body with edible glue.

9 Shape 10g (¼oz) of Soft Beige Sugar Dough into an oval for the head, push a spare skewer into the base and rest the head in the palm of your hand while you work on it. Use a ball tool to ease up the paste towards the middle of the face and bring out a small nose. Run your finger over any grooves in the paste and use the end of a paintbrush to indent the nostrils. Define the sides of the nose with a Dresden tool, then use a bone tool to indent eye sockets on either side of the nose.

10 Use a Dresden tool to make the mouth opening, then run a bone tool under it to bring out the bottom lip. Smooth over any grooves then push a bone tool into the corners of the mouth for the cheeks. Remove the skewer and attach the head to the skewered neck with edible glue.

11 Outline the eye sockets with a black food colour pen, adding a couple of fine eyelashes to each eye. Secure a small disc of White Sugar Dough inside each eye socket, then add two smaller discs of pale blue Sugar Dough on top. Add two tiny black discs for the pupils. Make a small

dent in each eye with a Dresden tool, brush with a little edible glue and add tiny white highlights. Draw on the eyebrows with a black food colour pen.

12 Roll two small balls of Soft Beige Sugar Dough for the ears, then brush a little edible glue on either side of the head level with the nose. Push the end of a bone tool into each ear and secure to the head, smoothing the paste over at the front of each ear.

13 Roll out 50g (1¾oz) of Red Sugar Dough and cut out the cloak shape following the size guide. Cut the sides at an angle so the cloak is narrower at the collar, then mark on creases with a Dresden tool. Brush around the back of the dress and neck with edible glue and attach the cloak. Gather it a little at the collar and leave the front of the cloak free from the dress. Press a Dresden tool around the top of the cloak to secure it to the neck.

14 Pinch out 5g (just under ¼oz) from 15g (½oz) of Golden Bear Brown Sugar Dough and roll into sausages for the long, side pieces of hair. Flatten them down and add texture with a Dresden tool. Attach to either side of the head with edible glue, tucking the ends in under the chin.

15 Divide the remaining 10g (¼oz) of Golden Bear Brown into one large piece and two small pieces for the fringe. Shape each piece into a cone, flatten slightly and texture with a Dresden tool. Attach to the front of the head with the larger piece on one side and the smaller pieces on the opposite side.

16 Roll out 15g (½oz) of Red Sugar Dough, cut out the curved hood following the size guide and mark on creases with a Dresden tool. Brush edible glue over the top of the head and along the top edge of the cloak. Attach the hood over the head, tuck in around the neck behind the hair and secure with a Dresden tool.

17 Brush edible glue around the skewer protruding from the arm and ease the basket into position using the pre-made hole. Hold in place until fully secured. Attach the second hand in the end of the sleeve and secure over the handle with edible glue.

LITTLE RED RIDING HOOD
SIZE GUIDE

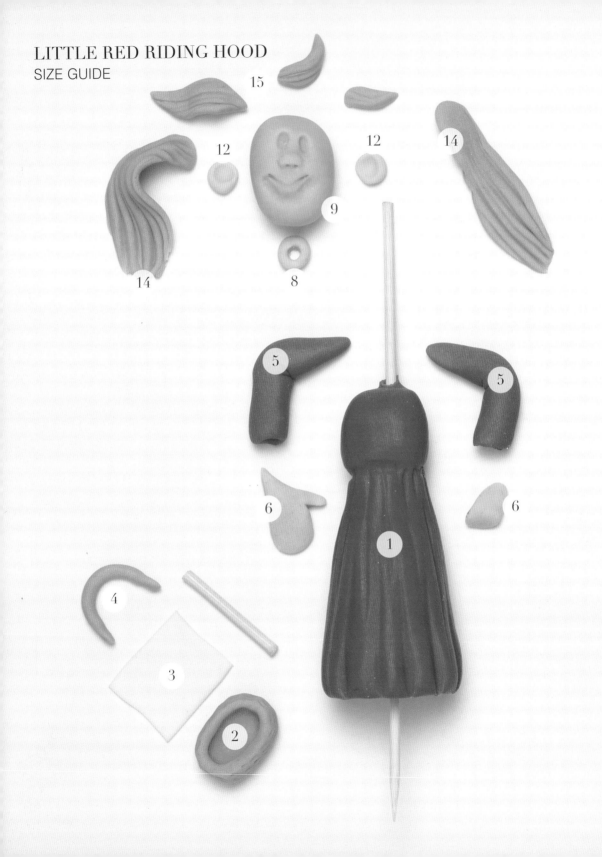

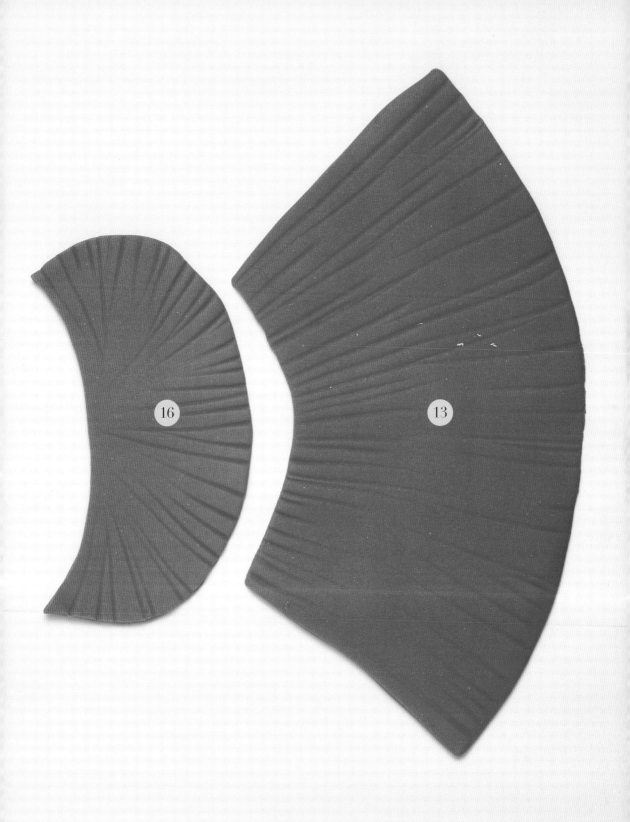

TEDDY BEARS' PICNIC

EDIBLES

60g (2oz) SK Ballerina Pink
Fairtrade Sugarpaste

SK Professional Food Colour
Pens: Black and Red

SK Sugar Dough:

170g (5¾oz) Golden Bear
Brown

30g (1oz) pale blue (White
+ pinch of Blue)

28g (1oz) White

25g (just over ¾oz) pink
(White + pinch of Red)

15g (½oz) cream (13g
(¼oz) White + 2g (⅛oz)
Golden Bear Brown)

2g (pinch) Black

2g (pinch) pale yellow
(White + Yellow)

2g (pinch) Red

Important note: Remember to remove the barbecue
skewers before the models are eaten.

EQUIPMENT

Basic equipment (see
pages 6 to 7)

15cm (6") square cake card
(optional)

5cm, 7cm and 7.5cm (2",
2¾" and 3") long wooden
barbecue skewers

Drinking straw

2.5cm and 3.5cm (1" and
1⅜") round cutters

Small ruler

Piping nozzle

PICNIC ITEMS

1 Roll out the Ballerina Pink sugarpaste, dampen the
cake card with a little cooled, boiled water and place
the sugarpaste over the top. Smooth over with a cake
smoother and trim any excess from the edges. Use the
edge of a small ruler to mark chequered lines across the
top then draw over them with a red food colour pen.

2 Use 8g (¼oz) of White Sugar Dough to make the
teapot, handle, spout and base following the size
guide. Attach the pieces together using edible glue then
push the wider end of a piping nozzle into the teapot lid to
mark a circle. Attach a tiny ball to the lid with edible glue.

3 Use 2g (pinch) of White Sugar Dough to make the
teacup, handle and base following the size guide.
Push the end of a bone tool into the top of the cup to open
it up a little then stick all the pieces together with edible
glue. Attach a small amount of cream Sugar Dough inside
the cup and texture the surface with the end of a paintbrush.
Set aside to dry.

4 Roll out 5g (just under ¼oz) of White Sugar Dough
then cut out two 3.5cm (1⅜") and three 2.5cm (1")

TEDDY BEARS' PICNIC
SIZE GUIDE

18

18

17

15

16

2

13

13

10

12

6

14

14

4

4

4

11

9

3

5

7

5

5

5

8

circles for the plates. Make small indents in each one with the end of a small rolling pin and set aside to dry.

5 For the cake, cut out two 2.5cm (1") circles from the cream Sugar Dough and one from Red Sugar Dough. Place the red disc between the cream discs and secure to a larger plate. Roll six small balls of Red Sugar Dough for the cherries and set aside. Make a disc from 3g (1/8oz) of White Sugar Dough for the icing, then make indents around the edge with a Dresden tool. Attach the icing and cherries to the top of the cake.

6 Roll 6g (just under 1/4oz) of White Sugar Dough into a sausage, flatten it down and cut out six triangles with a sharp knife. Run a red food colour pen around the middle of each triangle for the filling. Secure four sandwiches to a larger plate with edible glue and set aside to dry. Reserve the remaining two sandwiches for the bears.

7 Shape the straw from a thin sausage of White Sugar Dough and leave to dry.

8 Make a small sausage from 3g (1/8oz) of White Sugar Dough, flatten one end then push a bone tool into the other end to open up the glass. Secure a small amount of cream Sugar Dough inside the glass with edible glue, then push a Dresden tool into the top to make a hole for the straw. Draw stripes around the straw with a red food colour pen and attach inside the glass. Texture the surface of the cream Sugar Dough with the end of a paintbrush.

9 Shape 1g (small pinch) of White Sugar Dough into a cylinder for the baby's bottle. Shape a small sausage of Golden Bear Brown Sugar Dough for the teat and set aside. Make a small disc from Golden Bear Brown Sugar Dough and attach to the top of the bottle. Secure the teat on top with a little edible glue. Set aside to dry.

DADDY BEAR

10 For the lower body, roll 30g (1oz) of Golden Bear Brown Sugar Dough into a ball and push down to flatten it slightly, following the size guide.

11 Shape 8g (1/4oz) of Golden Bear Brown Sugar Dough into a cone to make a leg, push your thumb under the wider end and lift up the foot. Make another leg in the same way then attach them to either side of the body with edible glue and bring the feet together at the front.

12 Shape 20g (3/4oz) of pale blue Sugar Dough into a cone, pinch the paste between your finger and thumb to form a flat base so it will sit on top of the lower body. Pinch open the other end of the cone to fit the head inside. Mark the shirt opening with the blunt edge of a knife and push the end of a paintbrush into the paste to make three buttons. Push the 7.5cm (3") skewer centrally through the top and base of the body.

13 For the sleeves, shape 10g (1/4oz) of pale blue Sugar Dough into a sausage with tapered ends. Cut it in half, then push the end of a paintbrush into the thicker end of each sleeve. Mark the elbows with a Dresden tool and bend the arms slightly. Attach the arms around the shirt with edible glue, leaving enough room for the paws and a sandwich. Mark the shoulder area with a Dresden tool to secure the arms in place.

TEDDY BEARS' PICNIC
SIZE GUIDE

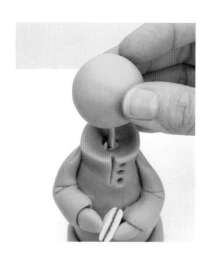

14 Shape 1g (small pinch) of Golden Bear Brown Sugar Dough into an oval for each paw and attach inside the sleeves with edible glue. Secure a sandwich between the paws as you attach them.

15 Roll 20g (¾oz) of Golden Bear Brown Sugar Dough into a ball for the head. Make a hole in the base of the head with a spare skewer and secure over the skewered body with edible glue.

16 Shape 4g (just under ¼oz) of cream Sugar Dough into a disc for the muzzle. Mark a central line with the blunt edge of a knife then push the end of a drinking straw into the paste on either side of the central mark at a 45° angle to make the mouth. Push a piece of spaghetti into the muzzle to make dimples. Attach the muzzle to the front of the head with edible glue and add eyes just above with a black food colour pen.

17 Roll a small ball of Black Sugar Dough, place your thumb and finger against the paste then pinch it with your other finger and thumb to form a pyramid-shaped nose. Attach to the top of the muzzle.

18 Divide 1g (small pinch) of Golden Bear Brown Sugar Dough into two equal balls for the ears then push a bone tool into each one to shape. Brush a little edible glue on either side of the head and attach the ears. Set aside to dry.

MUMMY BEAR

19 Shape the body from 20g (¾oz) of Golden Bear Brown Sugar Dough and make the legs in the same way as for Daddy Bear, using 7g (¼oz) for each leg. Secure the legs to the body with edible glue, bending one round slightly and leaving the other one straight.

20 Shape 20g (¾oz) of Pink Sugar Dough for the shirt in the same way as Daddy Bear, omitting the neck detail. Insert a 7cm (2¾") skewer through the shirt and body.

21 Roll a 1g (small pinch) ball of pink Sugar Dough for each sleeve and hollow out the base with a paintbrush handle. Attach them to the body with edible glue and secure in place with a Dresden tool.

22 For the collar, make a disc from 1g (small pinch) of pink Sugar Dough then make an indent in the front with a Dresden tool and smooth over. Make a hole in the centre with a spare skewer and attach over the skewered body with edible glue.

23 Shape 4g (just under ¼oz) of Golden Bear Brown Sugar Dough into a cone for each arm, mark the elbows with a Dresden tool and attach inside the sleeves. Bring the paws around the front of the body so they are almost touching and secure a sandwich on top.

24 Make the head and muzzle in the same way as Daddy Bear, using 15g (½oz) of Golden Bear Brown and 3g (⅛oz) of cream Sugar Dough. Make and attach the ears, nose and eyes in the same way as before.

BABY BEAR

25 Shape 16g (½oz) of Golden Bear Brown Sugar Dough into a cone and push a 5cm (2") skewer down the centre of the body.

26 Make the legs in the same way as for Daddy Bear, using 4g (just under ¼oz) for each leg. Mark the back of the knees with a Dresden tool, bend both legs inwards and secure to the body with edible glue.

27 Shape the bib, ties and neck from 2g (pinch) of pale yellow Sugar Dough following the size guide. Push a spare skewer through the disc to make a hole and secure over the skewered neck with edible glue. Attach the bib to the front of the body and the ties to the back with edible glue.

28 Make the arms in the same way as for Mummy Bear, using 3g (⅛oz) for each arm. Attach to the body with edible glue, resting one arm on the foot and the other in front of the body.

29 Make the head and muzzle in the same way as Daddy Bear, using 9g (¼oz) of Golden Bear Brown for the head and 1g (small pinch) of cream Sugar Dough for the muzzle. Make and attach the ears, nose and eyes in the same way as before, but make them a little bit smaller. Draw the letter 'B' on the bib with a black food colour pen. Leave to dry.

30 Position the bears and the picnic items on top of the covered cake card and secure in place with edible glue.

HUMPTY DUMPTY

————————————————————————

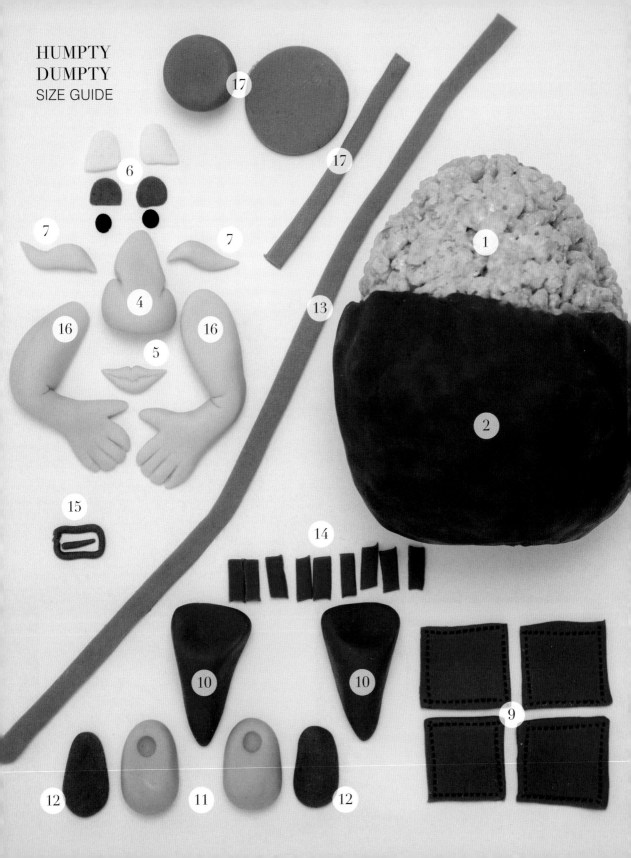

HUMPTY
DUMPTY
SIZE GUIDE

EDIBLES

90g (3oz) marshmallow rice cereal mix (see recipe on page 10)

SK Sugar Dough:

   90g (3oz) Blue

   70g (2½oz) Soft Beige

   25g (just over ¾oz) Golden Bear Brown

   3g (just under ¼oz) Brown

   1g (small pinch) Black

   1g (small pinch) Red

SK Red Professional Food Colour Pen

SK Pastel Pink Designer Dust Food Colour

EQUIPMENT

Basic equipment (see pages 6 to 7)

3cm (1⅛") round cutter

Stitching wheel modelling tool

1 Model the marshmallow rice cereal mix into the shape of Humpty Dumpty's body following the size guide (see page 10) and leave to cool completely.

2 Roll out 50g (1¾oz) of Blue Sugar Dough and stick it around the lower half of the body, smoothing over any creases with a cake smoother. Trim a neat edge across the top with a small knife. Mark two lines down the front with the blunt edge of a knife then run a stitching wheel alongside each line.

3 Roll out 45g (1½oz) of Soft Beige Sugar Dough and cover the top half of the body in the same way, trimming any excess where the paste meets the blue trousers.

4 Shape 6g (just under ¼oz) of Soft Beige Sugar Dough into a cone for the nose, following the size guide. Attach the nose to the head with edible glue and smooth over the paste at the join. Push a paintbrush handle into the base of the nose to make two nostrils and mark the sides of the nose with a Dresden tool.

5 Pinch a small amount of Soft Beige Sugar Dough into a mouth shape, following the size guide. Mark the lip line with a Dresden tool and attach to the head, smoothing the paste a little at the join. Draw lines around the mouth and nose and add dimples with a Dresden tool.

6 Flatten down two small balls of White Sugar Dough for the eyes, cut the bottoms straight and attach to the head with edible glue. Add two smaller discs of Brown Sugar Dough and two even smaller black discs on top. Outline the eyes with a very thin strip of Black Sugar Dough, then make and attach two thin black strips for the eyebrows. Make two very small dents in each pupil with a Dresden tool, brush with a little edible glue and use the Dresden tool to add two tiny white highlights to each one.

7 Divide 1g (small pinch) of Soft Beige Sugar Dough in half and make the eye bags following the size guide. Attach under the eyes and smooth the paste onto the head to secure.

8 For the waistband, roll 10g (¼oz) of Blue Sugar Dough into a long sausage then flatten down. Cut a strip long

enough to cover the seam between the pastes, secure in place with edible glue and trim to size.

9 Roll out 5g (just under ¼oz) of Blue Sugar Dough and cut out four 2.5cm (1") squares for the pockets. Run a stitching wheel around the edges and attach two at the front of the trousers and two at the back. Push a paintbrush handle into each of the corners.

10 Shape 8g (¼oz) of Blue Sugar Dough into a cone for each leg, following the size guide. Angle the larger ends to fit under the body and secure in place with edible glue.

11 Shape 4g (just under ¼oz) of Golden Bear Brown Sugar Dough into a pear shape for each foot, following the size guide.

12 Make the pear-shaped soles from 1g (small pinch) of Brown Sugar Dough for each one and flatten down. Attach to the underside of the shoes and mark the heels with the blunt edge of a knife. Secure the shoes to the end of each leg with edible glue.

13 Use 10g (¼oz) of Golden Bear Brown Sugar Dough to make a belt in the same way as the waistband, leaving a little overlap. Cut the end to a point and push a Dresden tool into one end of the belt to make six holes. Attach around the body with edible glue.

14 Roll out 5g (just under ¼oz) of Blue Sugar Dough and cut nine small strips for the belt loops, following the size guide. Attach over the belt with edible glue, smoothing over the joins.

15 Roll out 1g (small pinch) of Brown Sugar Dough into a long, thin sausage and cut a small section from the end. Shape the sausage into a rectangular buckle and attach to the front of the belt. Attach the small, brown section in the centre with edible glue.

16 Roll a 7g (just under ¼oz) sausage of Soft Beige Sugar Dough following the size guide. Flatten one end to make a hand, then make a cut in one side and bring out the thumb a little. Use a knife to make three marks for the fingers. Mark the elbows with a Dresden tool and bend. Attach to the side of the body with edible glue, resting the hand over the belt and smoothing over the paste. Repeat for the second arm, cutting the thumb in the opposite side and resting the hand slightly higher on the body.

17 Roll out 2g (just under ⅛oz) of Golden Bear Brown Sugar Dough and cut out a 3cm (1⅛") circle. Roll another 6g (just over ¼oz) of Golden Bear Brown Sugar Dough into a cylinder and attach to the disc with edible glue. Attach to the top of the head at an angle. Make a band to fit around the hat from 1g (small pinch) of Red Sugar Dough.

18 Colour the lips with a red food colour pen then use a damp paintbrush to soften the colour. Brush a small amount of pastel pink dust food colour over the cheeks.

OWL AND PUSSYCAT

EDIBLES

SK Sugar Dough:

65g (2¼oz) Golden Bear
Brown

65g (2¼oz) Orange

60g (2oz) Green

20g (¾oz) White

15g (½oz) Red

15g (½oz) teddy bear brown
(Golden Bear Brown Sugar
Dough + SK Teddy Bear
Brown Professional Paste
Food Colour)

6g (just under ¼oz) Blue

6g (just under ¼oz) Brown

1g (small pinch) Yellow

1g (small pinch) Black

1g (small pinch) pink (Red
+ White)

SK Teddy Bear Brown
Professional Paste Food Colour

SK Black Professional Food
Colour Pen

EQUIPMENT

Basic equipment (see
pages 6 to 7)

5cm wide x 7cm tall (2" x
2¾") polystyrene egg

3.5cm and 19cm (1³⁄₈" and
7½") long wooden barbecue
skewers

28-gauge floral wire: white

Important note: As this
figure is made using
inedible supports and wires,
remember to remove the
model from the cake before it
is served.

1 For the boat, shape 60g (2oz) of Green Sugar Dough into
a cone and open up the top with your thumbs, shaping
into a boat. Mark the wooden planks around the sides with the
blunt edge of a knife. Set aside.

2 Divide 6g (just under ¼oz) of Blue Sugar Dough into
10 balls. Roll each one into a tapered sausage then curl
up from the thicker end to make the waves, as shown in the
size guide. Attach five waves to either side of the boat with
edible glue.

OWL

3 To make the guitar, roll 1g (small pinch) of Brown Sugar
Dough into a sausage. Dip the end of the 3.5cm (1³⁄₈")
skewer into edible glue then push it into the sausage, leaving
1.5cm (⁵⁄₈") protruding from the end. Shape 5g (just under
¼oz) of Brown Sugar Dough into a pear shape, slightly flatten
it and squeeze a little in the middle. Push a bone tool into the
middle and make a hole in the top with a spare skewer. Attach
the covered skewer into the hole and set aside to dry. Draw on
some strings with a black food colour pen when dry.

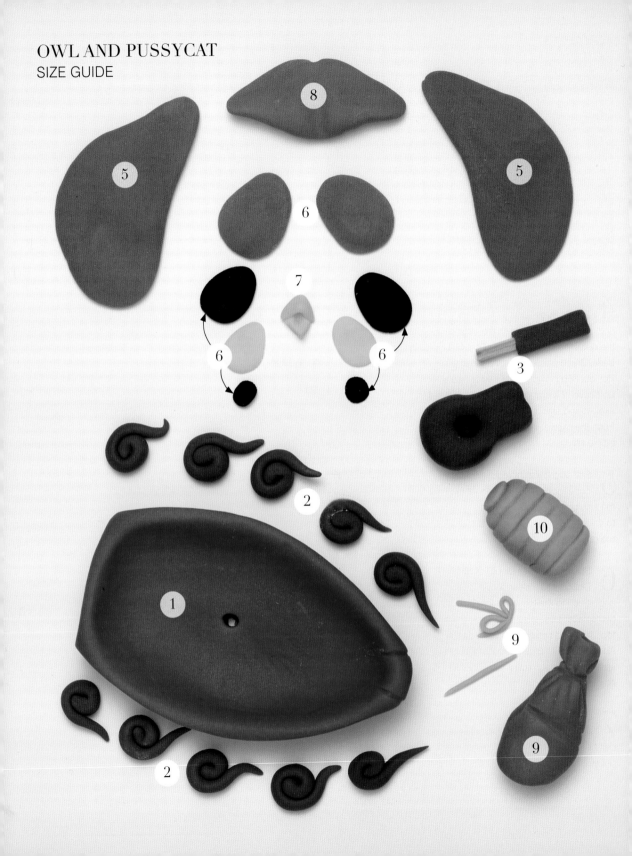

OWL AND PUSSYCAT
SIZE GUIDE

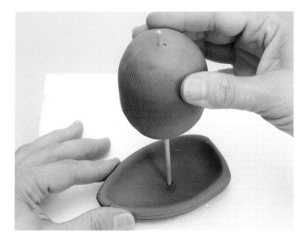
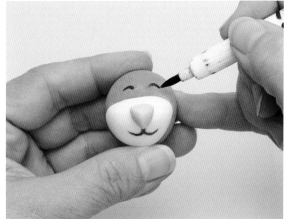

4 To make the owl, colour 60g (2oz) of Golden Bear Brown Sugar Dough with Teddy Bear Brown paste food colour. For the body, push the 19cm (7½") skewer down into the polystyrene egg, leaving 5cm (2") protruding from the base. Brush edible glue over the surface of the polystyrene. Roll out 35g (1¼oz) of the teddy bear brown Sugar Dough and cover the egg completely. Ease the paste around the skewer and smooth over the creases with a cake smoother. Push the skewer into the base of the boat and secure with edible glue.

5 Roll 10g (¼oz) of teddy bear brown Sugar Dough into a cone for each wing, then flatten and lengthen following the size guide. Attach the wings to either side and the guitar to the front of the body, then secure the wings to the front of the guitar with edible glue.

6 Shape 1g (small pinch) of teddy bear brown Sugar Dough into a pear shape for each eye, flatten down and attach to the top of the body with edible glue. Attach two smaller pear-shaped pieces of Black Sugar Dough on top, then add two smaller pieces of Yellow Sugar Dough. Add small balls of Black Sugar Dough for the pupils. Make a small dent in each eye with a Dresden tool, brush with a little edible glue and add tiny white highlights.

7 For the beak, shape a pinch of Yellow Sugar Dough into a triangle then push the end of a paintbrush into the centre to open it up. Mark the sides with a knife and attach between the eyes with edible glue.

8 To make the brow, shape 6g (just under ¼oz) of teddy bear brown Sugar Dough into a sausage with tapered ends, flatten it slightly then make an indent in the back with the side of a paintbrush. Attach the brow to the top of the head with edible glue.

9 Shape 10g (¼oz) of Red Sugar Dough into a cone for the money bag, mark around the sides with a Dresden tool and make an opening in the top with the end of a paintbrush. Mark on creases and make an indent just below the opening with a Dresden tool. Secure to the side of the boat with edible glue. Roll thin sausages from Golden Bear Brown Sugar Dough for the string and attach to the top of the bag.

10 Roll 10g (¼oz) of Golden Bear Brown Sugar Dough into a thick sausage for the honey-pot. Mark circles around it with the blunt edge of a knife and secure inside the boat with edible glue.

PUSSYCAT

11 Roll 2g (pinch) of Orange Sugar Dough into a ball for each front paw, then pinch one side between your finger and thumb to form a wedge. Mark four claws on the wider side with the blunt edge of a knife and secure both paws to the top of the owl's brow with edible glue.

12 Shape 8g (¼oz) of Orange Sugar Dough into a long cone for the tail and set aside. Shape 3g (⅛oz) of

PUSSYCAT
SIZE GUIDE

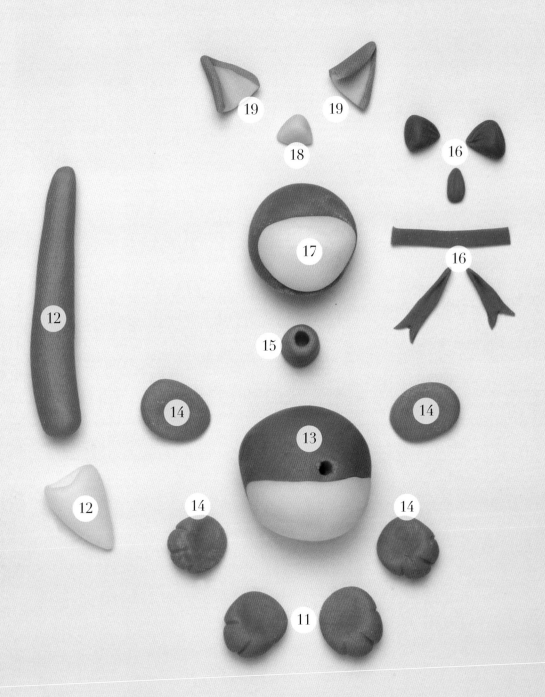

White Sugar Dough into a cone, push the end of a paintbrush into the wider end and open up the paste to fit the wider end of the tail inside. Secure to the end of the orange tail with edible glue and bring the white tip to a point between your fingers. Attach the tail to the top of the owl's head behind the brow and bend it to rest over the wing.

13 Roll 25g (just over ¾oz) of Orange Sugar Dough into a ball for the body and set aside. Roll 10g (¼oz) of White Sugar Dough into a ball, then flatten and attach it to the front of the body with edible glue. Push a spare skewer through the centre to make a hole, then push the body down over the skewer and secure to the front paws and tail with edible glue.

14 Make the back paws in the same way as the front paws using 3g (⅛oz) of Orange Sugar Dough for each one, then set aside. Make the legs in the same way as the paws using 2g (pinch) of Orange Sugar Dough for each one, but do not mark on claws. Secure the back paws to either side of the body, then position the legs just above them so they are angled slightly outwards.

15 Roll 2g (pinch) of Orange Sugar Dough into a ball for the neck, then push a spare skewer through the centre to make a hole. Attach the neck to the skewered body with edible glue, then gently squeeze the paste up the skewer to make the neck a little longer.

16 Roll out 3g (⅛oz) of Red Sugar Dough and cut out a strip to fit around the neck following the size guide, then attach in place with edible glue. Cut two more strips for the bow tails, cut a V-shape into the ends and pinch together at the top. Secure to the collar with edible glue. Pinch out a small section for the middle of the bow and set aside. Shape the remaining paste into two triangles for the bow loops, mark with a Dresden tool and attach in place. Secure a small sausage in the centre of the bow, tucking the ends under the triangles.

17 Roll 14g (½oz) of Orange Sugar Dough into a ball for the head. Make a hole in the paste using a spare skewer, then secure over the skewered neck with edible glue. Following the size guide, shape 4g (just under ¼oz) of White Sugar Dough into a muzzle that is thicker at the top, then attach to the head.

18 Roll a pinch of pink Sugar Dough into a ball, then pinch the paste with between your fingers and thumbs to form a pyramid-shaped nose. Secure to the top of the muzzle with edible glue. Draw on lines for the eyes and mouth with a black food colour pen.

19 Divide 1g (small pinch) of Orange Sugar Dough in half for the ears. Shape each piece into a triangle and set aside. Make two pink triangles in the same way. Attach the pink triangles over the orange ones with a little edible glue, press together and trim to size. Wrap each ear around the end of a paintbrush to shape them, then attach to the head with edible glue.

20 Cut a floral wire into six 1.5cm (⅝") lengths for the whiskers. Push three into each side of the muzzle, dipping the ends into edible glue first. Arrange them at slightly different angles. If you prefer not to use wires in your sugar models, draw on the whiskers instead using a black food colour pen.

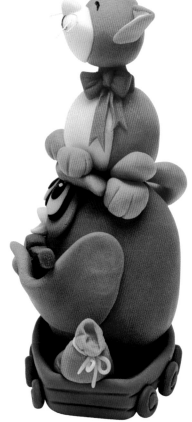

Other Books by Jan Clement-May

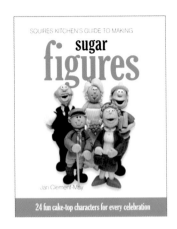

SQUIRES KITCHEN'S GUIDE TO MAKING

Sugar Animals

(B. Dutton Publishing, 2011)

Everyone has a favourite animal, and now you can create your very own edible replicas! Whether you make them for celebration cakes, cupcakes, cookies, gifts or just for fun, *Squires Kitchen's Guide to Making Sugar Animals* shows you how easy it is to get modelling.

Find out how to make dinosaurs, pets, aquatics and wild animals using Sugar Dough and just a handful of basic tools. Each model is photographed in full colour alongside a step-by-step picture and straightforward instructions – it couldn't be simpler! What's more, it's a great way to keep the little ones busy, either as a fun party activity or just for a rainy day.

If you're having a celebration and are looking for a fun and colourful centrepiece, you'll find a cake, cupcake or cookie project at the end of each theme. Recipes and equipment lists are provided, plus there are plenty of helpful hints for working with Sugar Dough.

SQUIRES KITCHEN'S GUIDE TO MAKING

Sugar Figures

(B. Dutton Publishing, 2012)

Where there's a celebration there's a cake! And what better way to decorate it than with fun and colourful figures made especially for the recipient.

Popular sugar artist, Jan Clement-May, shows you how easy it is to model and personalise figures in Sugar Dough using just a handful of basic tools. After explaining the essentials of modelling in sugar, she covers three popular subject matters – occupations, hobbies and celebrations – and presents an imaginative selection of figures within each chapter. So whether you're making a bride and groom for a wedding cake (complete with jolly vicar!), a cute baby boy or girl for a christening or baby's birthday, a cub scout or brownie for a children's party, or a cake for a sportsperson, this book is for you!

Plus, if you're looking to make party bag treats, wedding favours or if you're simply short of time, there are quick and easy cupcake designs to accompany every figure.

THE ART OF
SUGARCRAFT

by Squires Kitchen Tutors (B. Dutton Publishing, 2014)

AN AWARD-WINNING BOOK FROM THE WORLD-RENOWNED TUTORS AT SQUIRES KITCHEN

The Art of Sugarcraft is the only book of its kind to present a vast range of skills, techniques, projects and expert advice from 20 of the world's leading cake-decorating tutors. Ideal for keen cake makers, budding bakers and sugarcraft hobbyists of all abilities, it takes the reader through everything from basic recipes to masterclasses in sugarcraft, with everything in between.

This beautifully presented, fully illustrated book is divided into six chapters for ease of use: Baking and Patisserie; Chocolate; Foundation Sugarcraft; Extended Sugarcraft; Masterclasses; and Commercial Cake Decorating. Each section offers a broad range of traditional techniques, new skills and contemporary ideas – all with step-by-step instructions and photography – as well as projects to create at home, including celebration cakes and irresistible treats.

Each tutor offers a wealth of knowledge and individual style and all are leading names at Squires Kitchen, the oldest and one of the most popular schools of its kind in the UK. As one of the contributing tutors, Jan Clement-May shows you how to create a whole selection of unique sugar animals and presents a three-tier wedding cake featuring the complete bridal party modelled from Sugar Dough.

Squires Kitchen, UK
Squires House
3 Waverley Lane
Farnham
Surrey
GU9 8BB
0845 61 71 810
+44 (0) 1252 260 260
www.squires-shop.com

Squires Kitchen International School, UK
The Grange
Hones Yard
Farnham
Surrey
GU9 8BB
0845 61 71 810
+44 (0) 1252 260 260
www.squires-school.co.uk

For your nearest sugarcraft supplier, please contact customer@squires-shop.com.

B. Dutton Publishing is an award-winning publisher of cake decorating titles.
To find out more about our books, follow us at
www.facebook.com/bduttonpublishing and www.twitter.com/bduttonbooks.